The Appalachian Trail

by Ann and Myron Sutton

Steller of the North
Nature on the Rampage
Exploring with the Bartrams
Guarding the Treasured Lands: The Story of the
  National Park Service
Journey Into Ice: Sir John Franklin and the North-
  west Passage
Animals on the Move
The Life of the Desert
Among the Maya Ruins: The Adventures of John
  Lloyd Stephens and Frederick Catherwood

THE
APPALACHIAN TRAIL

Wilderness on the Doorstep

BY ANN AND MYRON SUTTON

with a foreword by
Stewart L. Udall

*We do not go into the woods to rough it; we go
to smooth it. We get it rough enough at home.*

Old Nessmuk   (GEORGE WASHINGTON SEARS)

J. B. LIPPINCOTT COMPANY
Philadelphia and New York

To Michael and Larry—and other
young hikers of today and tomorrow

All maps for The Appalachian Trail were created by Jean Tremblay.
Book design by Harry Eaby.
Permission for reproduction of the following quotations is gratefully
acknowledged:
Excerpts from Appalachian Trailway News, reprinted by permission
of the Appalachian Trail Conference.
Excerpts by Alberta Pierson Hannum, from The Great Smokies and
the Blue Ridge, reprinted by permission of the Vanguard Press, Inc.
"Trails," by Helen Frazee-Bower, reprinted by permission from the
March 1939, issue of Good Housekeeping Magazine, © 1939 by the
Hearst Corporation.
Excerpts from "The Road Not Taken" and from "New Hampshire"
from Complete Poems of Robert Frost. Copyright 1916, 1923 by Holt,
Rinehart and Winston, Inc. Copyright 1944, 1951 by Robert Frost.
Reprinted by permission of Holt, Rinehart and Winston, Inc.

Foreword

STEWART L. UDALL
Secretary of the Interior

In the nomenclature of modern America, there are certain words which have become almost as obsolete as the activities they define. One such is "walk." Another is "hike." From Madison Avenue to Madison, Wisconsin, from Portland, Maine, to Portland, Oregon, there is little doubt that it is more commonplace for boys to ask girls, men to ask women, and husbands to ask wives, to take a "ride" than a "stroll." And the summer silence of evenings fragrant with the breeze-borne scents of flowering fields, this, I am afraid, has all but disappeared as an experience both emotional and exhilarating. If one rides on a summer night in an air-conditioned car whose windows are up, then he inhales neither fumes nor fragrance. But if he tempts the evening in a convertible whose top is down, then, I fear, while he may see stars through the smog, his lot will be to smell noxious exhaust and not at all the sweetness of elemental nature.

Here and there, remarkably, however, swatches of green appear on the map, preserved through prescience, through the foresight of those who preferred grass to gas and pristine beauty to pavement hard. There still are enormous areas in the United States where one may indeed get away from it all, may find solitude, may walk among trees that were seedlings when our nation was born—or before—, may hike along paths whose wanderings over the hills and into the valleys are—unlike the highways—ungraded, unpasted, unguarded, unsullied, and uncongested.

"Can this be?" one asks himself when he first sets foot upon The Appalachian Trail. For it is not easy to believe one's eyes; it is difficult for the imagination to accept the staggering notion that here is a footpath, within a day's drive or less of 60 per cent of our nation's population, a footpath from Georgia to Maine—two thousands miles in length. The mere thought of it creates a reverential mood: What, all this God among mankind?

But it is so! Here it is, close to men, a protected wilderness traversing the teeming East Coast of America. Some have hiked its length in a single season; some have done it by piecing it together—a stretch one year, a stretch the next; and some, unable to do its entirety, have sampled its flavor, and have returned with the wings of fancy when their feet were elsewhere planted. And there is something undeniable: None who has seen it has not marveled; none who has traveled its great length has not been moved.

The Appalachian Trail is first of all upon you as a physical experience. It can be overwhelming as a valley opens its face at a turn in the path. It can be delicate as a cold and shimmering stream. It can be subtle and surprising as the chipmunk darts between the rocks, as the cardinal flashes through the trees.

The Trail is an historical experience: One realizes that it was crossed by Daniel Boone and used by pioneers. It is a poetic reminder of Whitman and Frost. It is a philosophical treatise suggestive of Emerson and Thoreau.

All this is here, captured and conveyed by Ann and Myron Sutton, two young lovers of the wilderness. Their words give us something of the wonderment, their photographs something of the presence, of The Appalachian Trail. But, most of all, this—their book—provides us with a glimpse of an American treasure that is threatened. For 866 miles of the Trail, a stretch here, a stretch there, are segments by sufferance. They cross private lands whose owners in so many cases have given only oral permission; and thus, a major portion of this magnificent natural and national heritage is constantly subject to the whim of individuals, and to the vagaries of urban development and commercial exploitation.

So this book is far more than a statement of what is; it also is a calling out for what must be. And what must be is simply this: the incorporation of the full length of The Appalachian Trail into a protected, unbroken chain forged by local, State, and Federal agencies.

It has been said that "A voyage of a thousand miles begins with but a single step." Now it must be said—and the Suttons have said it—that the veneration and viability of the two thousand miles of The Appalachian Trail, as a national legacy to be nourished and kept alive for future generations, that this must begin with but two important steps: (1) Appreciation and (2) Action.

This book gives us the appreciation.

Now we must provide the action.

Washington, D. C.
January 1967

Contents

Acknowledgments

Officials of the Appalachian Trail Conference have given unstintingly of help and advice in the preparation of this book. Stanley A. Murray, Conference Chairman, and Jean C. Stephenson, Editor-in-Chief, read the manuscript in its entirety and made many valuable suggestions, for which we are deeply grateful. Any remaining errors of fact or interpretations are ours.

The entire manuscript was also read and corrected by Stan Young and Bart Hague of the Bureau of Outdoor Recreation, and by Fred M. Packard, of the National Park Service, United States Department of the Interior. These gentlemen rendered assistance beyond the call of duty. Portions of the text were reviewed by Arthur Stupka and Ross Bender, of Great Smoky Mountains National Park, Joseph McManus, of Palisades Interstate Park, and C. F. Belcher, of the Appalachian Mountain Club. These persons corrected a number of errors and impressions, and helped in many ways to refine the manuscript—for which, again, the final responsibility is ours.

The following individuals and organizations have also been of assistance: Sam P. Weems, Maurice Broun, Tom Campbell, M. Woodbridge Williams, Courtland T. Reid, Brian O'Neill, Stig Lundberg, Otto Wigardt, Bertil Haglund, Mervyn Bell, E. J. S. Burbidge, R. J. Labuschagne, and Antti Haapanen; Forest Service, U.S. Department of Agriculture, Georgia Department of Industry and Trade, Virginia Department of Conservation and Economic Development, New Hampshire Department of Resources and Economic Development, Svenska Turistföreningen, National Parks Commission of England and Wales, and the Library of Congress.

Special thanks are due Robert D. Mead, of J. B. Lippincott Company, good hiking companion and champion of the wilderness, for advice and counsel throughout.

Ann and Myron Sutton

Introduction

If a hundred authors described The Appalachian Trail, no two of their books would be alike. Every trip, every experience, every day on the Trail is different. Not only is the mountain environment complex geologically and biologically; it changes hour by hour, season by season, and year after year. Although we have included a number of facts to try to give the Trail—and our own experiences on it—some kind of meaning, fuller details such as mileages, shelters, side trails, history, fauna and flora are available in publications of the Appalachian Trail Conference and associated organizations (listed in Appendix II), and in the specialized literature (see the Bibliography).

We are more concerned with walking itself, with walking along this particular trail, and with the role of this trail and all trails in the structure of modern society.

As a prototype, The Appalachian Trail has its uniqueness, but it also has a distinct objective: to serve in a very special way the people who live near it, and some who live not so near. If it is to be complete, and indeed survive, it must succeed in this also. The danger is that it could be destroyed or severely damaged because it is a wilderness trail and wilderness is fragile. It has already been destroyed in numerous places, and then repaired. Some day, if we run out of wilderness, there will be nothing left to repair it with.

A great many people are determined to see this trail preserved, and are determined to preserve others like it, even if that means a limit to housing developments, a "no" to chairlift proposals, and a taming of superpassions for parkways and interstate highways impinging upon scenic lands of unquestioned integrity.

Because it exists as a slim thread of wilderness in a spreading urban society, The Appalachian Trail is a symbol and a promise. It is a place for quiet walking and meditation in the midst of natural beauty. Furthermore, it is a human enterprise of enormous proportion, descended from men and women in the past whose walks in this region have made history or who have left behind momentous thoughts that walking inspired in them. And in time we, the human beings of the present, are expected to hand over the Trail to our descendants in better condition than we got it ourselves. All these things are what this book is about.

As it exists today, the Trail is a place where beauty, solitude and personal discovery combine to produce some of the most exciting aspects of hiking in North America today. The Trail is not easy. It was never meant to be. At times and in certain places its branches slap your face and unload drops of moisture on you. Its rocks and roots may trip you, and its cobwebs cover your eyes. Its heat stifles, its cold freezes, its lightning become intimate, its midges and mosquitoes inflict sharp wounds, and its chiggers are merciless.

But those who believe in the wilderness—and understand it—accept all this and work relentlessly to keep the Trail environment exactly the way it is. Men and women who have hauled their axes and marking materials miles into the woods to keep the Trail open, and people who in distant places have joined the battle against air and water pollution, have in their own ways striven to maintain the Trail and its environment. Its founders intended The Appalachian Trail to be a footpath through the wilderness. Nothing more. And he who hikes the Trail is apt to discover some surprising things about the mountains, the wildlife—and himself.

The need of our times is to understand The Appalachian Trail precisely and fully, for it is a precedent setter and has to be right. It has to be managed properly, also. Its purpose of being a simple footpath through the wilderness must be clearly kept in mind by the public whose support is so essential to its preservation.

The temptation in a book about the Trail is to devote the greatest number of pages to the greatest scenic wonders, thus giving 40 per cent of the book to the Great Smokies and 40 per cent to the White Mountains—and let the rest fall where it may. But this is not a book about scenery alone or about spectacle. It is about hiking, largely regional hiking, along the whole Appalachian Trail, and the Great Smokies and White Mountains each constitute less than 4 per cent of the total distance. The rest is lesser known— and there are marvelous discoveries to be made.

One of these discoveries is a deceptive one that is easily overlooked in its simplicity. The Trail is an entity of public and private hope—public because its establishment and perpetuation represent a curious maturity of civilization, and private because the average hiker still has certain portions of the Trail he's never seen and wants to hike as soon as he can.

We have not seen enough of the Mahoosucs or the Barren-Chairback range, and certainly have it in our plans to explore some future day the length of the Chattahoochee Forest. When the sun comes north again and the birch leaves come out to a glowing green, we intend to head for New Hampshire and hike some more in that wild wonderland known as the White Mountains. There are also places already familiar to which we want to return as often as we possibly can.

This is hope. A great deal of excitement and adventure and new discovery awaits us on the Trail; we know that. And in the winter days and long cold nights our hearts are warmed with dreams of days on the Trail and in the mountains—a warmth and a refreshment that last as long as life itself.

A century ago, Henry David Thoreau said, "We have advanced by leaps to the Pacific, and left many a lesser Oregon and California unexplored behind us."

The time has come to explore them—and the Trail is waiting.

Alexandria, Virginia   Ann and Myron Sutton

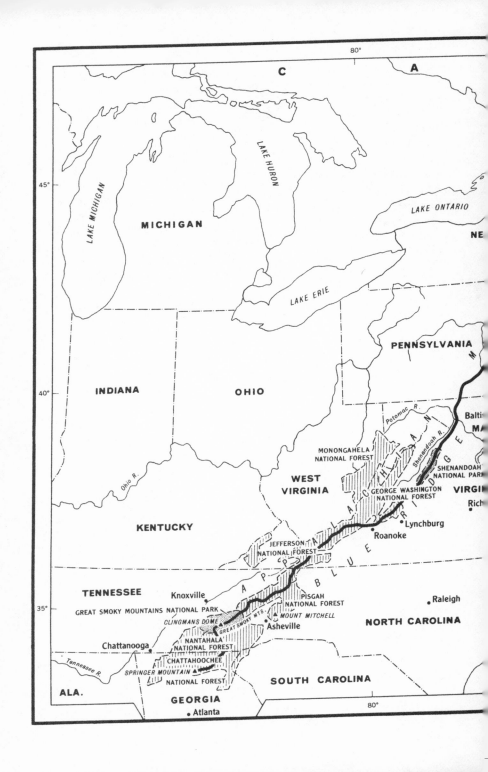

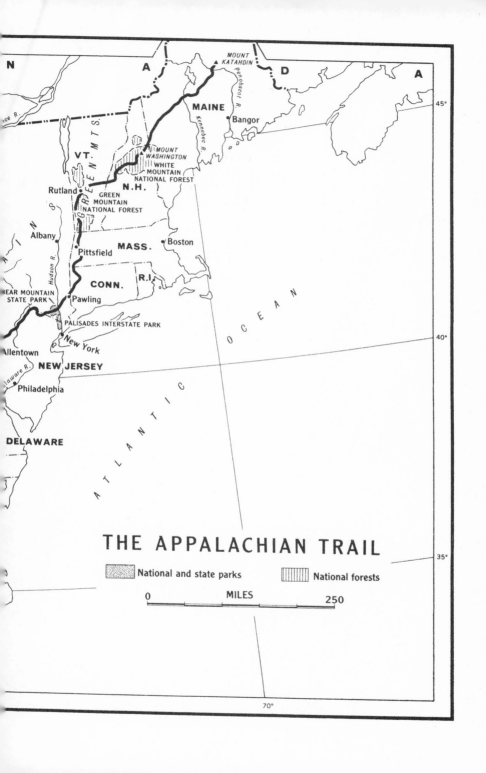

THE APPALACHIAN TRAIL

National and state parks   National forests

MILES

0   250

1

There is no orthodoxy in Walking. It is a land of many paths and no-paths, where every one goes his own way and is right.

Trevelyan

The Cloud Path

Not far from the village of Eckville, Pennsylvania, there is an old dirt road that winds up the slopes of a wooded valley. It is not much of a road any more, and perhaps never was. You cannot drive over it. There are cuts across it where streams have flowed in and out for a good many years. And the grade is too steep and rocky in places for modern cars.

Time has forgotten how many years have passed since logging trucks —or logging wagons—rolled down those grades. You can still hear tales in this country of wood-burning sites that once blazed in the vicinity and furnished charcoal for early pig-iron furnaces.

About all the old road is fit for now is to walk on, and even that is a little tricky. There are boulders in the way that have rolled down the slopes from some forgotten stream bed, and lie ready to trip you if you do not watch where you place your boots.

Nevertheless, the old road is passable and fairly long, and like so many long old roads, it leads to an interesting destination. Or more correctly, it leads to several destinations.

For one thing, it reaches the top of the ridge, a not altogether simple accomplishment. The number of wild and wooded ridges remaining in the world each year is smaller than it was the year before, the net loss having been expended for "Mountain View Cottages" or "Hillcrest Estates" or radar stations. Therefore, the tackling and climbing of this one represents a social as well as physical achievement because one does not have to violate the laws of trespass.

Moreover, reaching the top of the ridge is something of a blessing for another reason. The climb has been a long and tiring one, enough to bring an average walker to his first rest stop. To be sure, this is not the conquest of Kanchenjunga or Everest; this ridge is probably not 1/29 the height of those. Yet it is a height, of sorts, and quite possibly a large percentage of persons who climb it are not trained or conditioned to do any climbing at all. These people, then, will welcome the chance to stop and rest.

We walked along that road and up that ridge one autumn morning when the dew was fresh and the fallen leaves still damp and cold from the night air. Rays of sunshine slanted into the forest like beams from spotlights, each picking out a leaf, a rock, a patch of bark, a trickling stream as something to be prized and cherished and applauded for having put on a sterling performance. We were not in a hurry. We walked slowly—with good weather and good friends—intending to see as much as we could in these Pennsylvania mountains.

The road was not much better on top of the ridge, but because the water from rains runs off less rapidly than below, there were in places growths of moss that added a touch of carpetry to the walking.

And then, a short distance farther on, we came to a point where the old road was intersected by a trail; at one side was a weathered sign that read "The Pinnacle, 2.8."

Less than a mile along the trail to the Pinnacle we came to a widening in the woods—an open glade inviting us to stop and rest. A few steps down from that, through the trees and into a shady cove that looked as if it had been undisturbed or even untouched for years, was a spring.

With the abundance of old roads wandering through these woods, is seemed fairly obvious that the spring had been known and used and disturbed for generations. But that in turn appeared to have been a long time ago, and now another forest was growing up around the spring. Very little evidence of former use—or misuse—remained; the spring and the forest were reverting to a natural state.

Not having a drinking cup we found a broad oak leaf, rolled it into a cone-shaped container, and dipped it into the pool. The water was perfectly clear and so cold that we could not drink as rapidly as we wanted. But in time our thirst was satisfied and we moved on toward the Pinnacle.

The old logging roads gave out entirely. Passage became confined and the trail less smooth as we neared the point of the ridge. How welcome was this change of tactile values. The rough road had become a rough trail and in the final stages there was no trail at all, the route being simply from blaze to blaze among the trees, or from one paint mark to another on the jagged rocks. We had by stages retrogressed—or if you prefer, progressed—from Eckville's highway to rough dirt road to abandoned road to trail to wilderness.

At the end of 2.8 miles, the Pinnacle, a rocky terminus of the ridge on which we had walked, came into view through the trees, and in another moment we broke out of the forest onto a rocky ledge and our first commanding vista of the day.

There were the Appalachians all right! You could single them out among a thousand mountains. Ridges and valleys merged with more ridges and more valleys, lost in the distance in a deepening haze. Dark evergreens and gray-stemmed blankets of naked deciduous trees covered the ridges; in the vales lay farmlands of dry grass or bare sod.

But a moment's observation was enough. For hungry hikers, scenery is best combined with food.

We spent no time in selecting a site to eat; we sat down where we were, slipped off our packs and opened a trail lunch on the rocks.

Our appetites told us that it had been a long time since we had started out that morning. Time had flown rapidly and strength of appetite was the only measure of time we knew or wanted. We had thrust ourselves into the Appalachian wilderness and had climbed into some of the oldest mountains on earth. We had given up our sense of time, and with that our sense of hurry.

In view of this, it seemed as though we had come a thousand miles through wild forest and leaf-strewn glades to get here. We could have. We were almost exactly in the center of this long and undulating chain of Appalachians. It was more than a thousand miles to the north by trail where those mountains ended in Canada and more than a thousand miles south to the lowering foothills of Georgia.

Suddenly, as we sliced the foil from a bar of concentrated pork and beef, a turkey vulture skimmed the edge of the trees and soared out over the void of haze and distance below. Free as the air, our spirits soared likewise. The very act of coming near these mountains produced a special exhilarating effect. For twenty years we had been in and out of the Appalachians. We had hiked or camped in this and nearly every other part of them, swum in the streams, walked through the golden forests of autumn, and stood on the summits in the cold of a winter night, watching the aurora paint the sky with red and green.

The mountains had remained as old and as new as the first time we had seen them—and each time our rediscovery must have been akin to that of De Soto who, seeing the southern ramparts of these mountains, had named them after the Apalachees, a tribe of Muskhogean Indians on the coast of the Gulf of Mexico.

De Soto could not have dreamed how much of a mountain range he had found. Appalachia is big country, immense country. There must be a thousand "Pinnacles" or more.

Altogether, the Appalachians sprawl over 17 degrees of the curvature of the earth, not much to an astronaut but a fair distance for a crow, and from their summits one can look out over fully 100,000 square miles of scenery.

As the mountain men would say, that is a heap o' landscape.

From the southernmost knob at latitude 33 degrees north to the sea at 50 degrees, the Appalachians curve and twist into every conceivable form, and rise from zero to 6,684 feet above sea level.

All this provides a terrain so varied and so spread out that an enormous sweep of climate occurs. A day like this at the Pinnacle, with the ridges brushed by a lukewarm breeze, seems characteristic of summer and autumn days. Yet the Appalachians remain anything but constant when it comes to climate. Their gentle grandeur deceives. Air drafts are tricky. Storms are treacherous. One day will be glorious, the next gloomy. As a matter of fact, some northern parts of the range possess what local residents describe, without a trace of despair, as the worst weather in the world.

A hiker sitting here at the Pinnacle, or at any other overlook on a sunlit autumn afternoon, can hardly credit the stories he hears. He can hardly begin to guess what massive variations these mountains hold. If he climbs to the crest of any ridge from Maine to Georgia, he sees in the softly sloping ridges and winding valleys only a suggestion of what such a vast diversity of latitude and climate has wrought.

To see it fully, to understand it, to revel in it he cannot merely sit —or ride. He must get out and walk. By walking he comes sufficiently close and moves with sufficient slowness to perceive the one thing that is constant in the Appalachians: variation. And if there is a common denominator by which these ranges are judged, it is the consequent variation of plant and animal life that make them the most living, enduring mountains of all. Mountains have specialties, and that of the Appalachians is life.

Native naturalists, with an edge of pride in their voices, claim almost as many species of trees as in Europe, and can show you many a tree that reaches the highest crown and greatest girth of its kind. They will take you on trails through wildflower displays that contain more blossoms than two human eyes can see in a single season or a dozen seasons. Great numbers of persons come to see the flowering rhododendrons, but out in the meadows, deep in the woods, and high on the ridges, there are less conspicuous displays, such as the dozens of species of orchids from Maine to Georgia.

Off on your own on a quiet trail, your eyes may behold animals that vary from the tiny colorful salamanders of the Great Smoky Mountains (red-backed salamanders occupy the whole Appalachians) to the bear and elk of the Blue Ridge, from ravens on the ridges to hawks at Hawk Mountain (the ridge behind where we sit), and from mice to moose in the Maine woods. Spruce-fir forests resembling those in Canada come all the way down to Tennessee on the crests of the Appalachians, so one finds birds in these southern states that are characteristic of much more northerly lands. There are reptiles in plenty, too, though poisonous snakes are rarely encountered, and at the right time of year certain insects give notice of their abundance, particularly gnats, mosquitoes, black flies, ticks and chiggers. It is all part of a woods environment the richness of which is rarely paralleled anywhere else in the temperate zone.

John Muir called the Sierras a "Range of Light." Had he seen more of the Appalachians, he might have called them a "Range of Life."

Abundance, the essence of it all, shows up in the forests, the meadows, the wetlands. The mountains are like an ocean—full of life and action that may not be immediately evident but can be discovered and rediscovered perpetually because so much is changing and so much is new. Such an ocean of wooded, waving, swelling mountain beauty and grandeur, Muir once wrote of the Appalachians, is not to be described. Perhaps not. But it is certainly to be enjoyed, no matter what the season.

"I prefer winter," a farmer near Orwigsburg had said to us that morning, "when the snow comes deep across those fields up yonder and the land is as white and pure as it ever gets."

The fields "up yonder" were now "down yonder"—the land of the Pennsylvania Dutch. Each Appalachian region, besides its blanket of natural life, wears also a mantle of human influence. In this region at the center of the range are the traditional hex symbols and a people gifted for hospitality. Like the New Englander, the north woodsman or the southern highlander, these people are provincial and individual. And so it has been since man first came into these hills.

There has not been an era of human history on this continent that has not been burned into the Appalachians, nor of which some durable mark does not remain. Even such as Colonel Daniel Boone, who rarely

The authors and their party at lunch on The Pinnacle, near Hawk Mountain in Pennsylvania, a relatively inaccessible and hence unspoiled area near the Trail.

A sign on Mount Adams in New Hampshire's Presidential Range warns hikers of the dangers of the weather.

PRECEDING PAGE: High clouds and mist in the Great Smoky Mountains of North Carolina and Tennessee

In picturesque New Hampshire, The Appalachian Trail skirts Lonesome Lake and rises along the crest of Mount Lafayette.

had time to see with an artist's eye the land he was driving a wedge of settlement into, could now and then look around "with astonishing delight" and behold "the ample plains and beauteous tracts below."

All up and down the Appalachians lies layer upon layer of history, like a stratigraphic column: the Indian layer at the bottom; the layer of Indian wars; the hungry-settler layer; the social-and-political layer; the poverty-versus-industry layer; the desolation and regeneration.

It has been more than 130 years since Thoreau climbed Mount Katahdin in Maine, and over 100 years since Muir "spent some joyous time" on a thousand-mile walk to the Gulf.

And it has been less than sixty years since a schoolteacher was dismissed in the heart of the mountains for teaching that the world was round. Or less than that since the Scopes trial. As the geographer said, this is a land where a man is a man and not a monkey.

But time changes the land and inevitably the men as well, and in many ways that is a shame. There was a peculiar spontaneity about the original Appalachian Mountain people, a zest for life that is being altered.

The mountain men of the Appalachians had, and some still have, a dialect distinct enough to be their own, as when they give directions: "Go across Wolf and Coon to the headwaters of Cutshin; down Cutshin, fording three times; up Flacky, across a right rough little hill to the head of Owl's Nest; down Owl's Nest to Middle Fork, and up Middle Fork a piece to a deep ford; ford the river, and you are at the place you are aiming at."

Wherever you aim at—if you can get there—the Appalachians have something arresting to reveal in every kingdom—animal, vegetable and mineral. Large parts of the mountains have been "opened" by highways, as here in the Eckville region; and where roads do not reach, there are likely to be trails that do, such as the trail to the Pinnacle. It seems safe to say that nearly every square mile of the Appalachians can be reached by some form of passage: highway, fire road, railroad, river or trail.

Highways generally link the cities, neglecting the mountains. But there are some notable exceptions. The Blue Ridge Parkway and the Skyline Drive, for example, form a single continuous mountain roadway, joining together 600 miles of ridgetop from northern Virginia to the Great Smoky Mountains.

But this is only a fourth of the Appalachians. The rest, in addition to this section, is tied by means of a mountain-to-mountain link that is not a highway, not an airline system, not even a communications network. It is not political or biological, and in some respects, not even social. It is simply an unobtrusive wilderness pathway.

Just who had the first idea for a "long trail" is hard to say. The early Indians had many extended trails, as we shall see. A man named James Taylor, of Vermont, suggested a wilderness "long trail" the length of Vermont, and the Green Mountain Club was organized in 1910 to clear and mark its 250 miles.

In the early 1900's a man named Benton MacKaye dreamed about and then proposed that an even longer wilderness trail be established in the "Appalachian Domain." It would be, for all practical purposes, an endless trail, accessible to great numbers of people in the heavily populated eastern United States.

The idea struck a spark and a mile was cleared, a marker designed and some scouting done. Then it lay fallow for a time. In 1926, Arthur Perkins, of Hartford, revived the project. Now the time was ripe and the idea spread like wildfire on a dry ridge. Existing trail systems were incorporated and new paths pushed through the woods as fast as volunteer groups and their leaders could lay them out and blaze them.

The result is the largest system of trails anywhere, a series of marked footpaths connecting summit to summit, forest to forest, river to river, and era to era.

Dominating this system is a single trail 2,000 miles in length—sometimes a wide path through the high cloud forest, sometimes a narrow tunnel in thickets of laurel, sometimes only a stretch of bare gray rock on a mountaintop.

From the summit of Springer Mountain in Georgia to the summit of

Katahdin in Maine, this high trail winds through a wild Appalachian paradise. Could it be called anything less than "The Appalachian Trail"? Like John Muir's wilderness, it is almost not to be described. It is so long and varied, so subject to changing moods and changing physiography, that hardly anybody knows it well. Few people have hiked the length of it, and they cannot be expected to remember every one of the nearly five million footsteps they took in order to cover it all.

For the most part, The Appalachian Trail, or "A.T." as it is known for short, is a unique recreational asset of prime value to day-use hikers. These are the one-shotters, the newcomers, the week-enders, the short-termers. And there are those who come as we came to Eckville and parked our car and started up the old log road.

In elevation, The Appalachian Trail varies from tidewater to 6,642 feet. It crosses portions of fourteen states, and is nowhere farther than one day's drive from 120 million people.

Yet a wilderness trail it was intended to be, and a wilderness trail it is, to the best of the ability of the hundred or so trail clubs who fight to save it and work to maintain it. Thousands of volunteer laborers and hikers clean it and clear it where necessary. Thus it is kept more or less in a state of perpetual readiness for any one or more of the 120 million people it threads its way through—to get away from the others.

If that seems a paradox, it is only the first of many. The Trail itself is a collection of paradoxes. It is extraordinarily long—but its greatest use is short-term, short-distance walking. It goes through lands characterized by beautiful weather and by weather almost as miserable as any on earth. In places it is a superbly constructed trail—in others there has been no construction whatever, and the hiker scrambles as best he can over fallen timbers, soggy swamps or bare rock, following white-paint blazes as a matter of survival.

No matter the paradoxes. When you smell the wild forest and feel the wind against your face, the time has come to get out on the trail. The blazes point the way and the spirit god of hikers whispers, "Go, thou restless soul, into the woods of the mountains. Take with you any problem, or trouble, or worry. *Solvitur ambulando!* It is solved by walking!"

We finished lunch and tidied up the portion of the Pinnacle that we had occupied, then explored the cracks and crevices and caves of the ledges before departing. The boys, lost in underground exploration, were reluctant to leave, but we had to get around to Pulpit Rock and Windsor Furnace Road before we could retrace our steps to Eckville.

This took steady walking. As daylight faded we followed the familiar blazes of The Appalachian Trail, here laid out along the old dirt roads where logs of the original forest had been hauled away to charcoal furnaces or sawmills or homes. It was cool evening when we started to descend along the slope where the boulders lie in the path to trip the careless hiker.

A moon had risen, nearly full, half-hidden by a bank of clouds in the east. An evening breeze was stirring the leaves in the forest, but not very much. The air was moist again, and the fallen leaves were growing damp and cold in the evening air.

There would be rain by morning, and the cloud path, The Appalachian Trail up there behind us in the darkness and ahead across the forested basin, would be glistening with moisture.

Back in the woods and high on the slopes of the mountain came the faint but unmistakable call of an owl. We slowed down for a moment and, walking as silently as we could, listened. It came again.

2

*These ridges is might' nigh straight up and down,
and, as the feller said, perpendic'lar.*

Quoted by Horace Kephart

Mountains and Mountain Men

The rain had ended yesterday. It had been one of those seemingly perpetual drenching rains of spring for which the Great Smoky Mountains are known. Heavy fog and mist had hidden everything but the nearest trees.

Now the haze of the mountains had been wiped away as if by a sponge in a single imperious stroke. Mount Le Conte, breaking off to the west along a gently climbing ridge, rose up in its forest cloak as if it were a Maya chieftain, on some celestial scale rising in the morning sun to Kukulcan. Le Conte had always had that regality; it was a master peak, and especially so today, uncapped by stratus cloud and free of fog. It was not the highest Appalachian peak; regality is rarely synonomous with height in the Appalachians, for most peaks are connected with others or with ridges. Altogether, 350 peaks and 350 miles of ridgetop are above 5,000 feet in elevation. Le Conte was one of the rare partly disengaged mountains, majestic in its semidetachment.

Down across Thomas Divide, we could see, as we hiked The Appalachian Trail north of Newfound Gap, the silver surface of Fontana Reservoir, a dozen miles away. Along Soco Creek and the Oconaluftee

River, where the Cherokees had lived for centuries, a smoke rose lazily here and there. To the east, Balsam Mountain appeared as a crest on an ocean of ridges and summits.

We were surrounded by mountains, and all of them were at once strange and familiar. Here were the Rockies, the Cascades and Sierras, the Central American and Hawaiian volcanoes, Mount Cook in New Zealand, Kosciusko in Australia, Uludag in Turkey, Khao Yai in Thailand, the Olympics, Alps and Andes all wrapped together. We'd seen them all, and here they were again, each embodied in one way or another in the Appalachians.

The only difference was that the Appalachians were easy to get to from where we lived, and easy to hike through, thanks to a skyline trail from peak to peak for 2,000 miles.

Away from those peaks and their Appalachian Trail system, or riding by as a motorist, it is almost impossible to imagine the enormous extent of life in the forests, or to guess how many sounds of active, living creatures one can hear on an Appalachian summit in spring. The hiker hears them all, and unless he is a proficient naturalist they are far more than he can identify or separate. What a "Range of Life" indeed!

On this special morning we had not embarked upon a search for any particular sounds. In such an abundance of sound and sight and odor one does not so much search as try to sort what one sees and hears and smells.

Everything crowded upon us: assorted animal voices, water dripping from leaves, a rivulet singing, the odor of a rainwashed forest, a fresh morning breeze through fir boughs. The solid earth felt good beneath our feet, and the familiar whacking sound of our hiking boots against the rocks came as music to our ears.

We stopped and knelt to photograph a painted trillium in seclusion. Not all of the leaves of trees had come out yet, and the new ones bursting from their buds had so delicate a shade of green or brown or red as to impart to this forest a likeness to the Garden of Eden.

Around the next bend we walked straightaway into a pocket of spruce and fir. There was far less light in this densely clustered grove of trees, but the richness of the forest floor could hardly be concealed. Soil, roots, rocks, logs and fallen limbs were nearly covered with a reddish-brown mulch and dark peaty humus. From this was beginning to grow a blanket of young green ferns and other plants, including the tiny ubiquitous oxalis, or common wood sorrel. At one point a speck of sunlight touched an oxalis flower, enhancing the brilliance of its magenta-lined white petals and delicate yellow centers, reminding us of a candle in the gloom.

Ostensibly we were aimed for The Jump-off, but on The Appalachian Trail one need not always aim for a particular rendezvous. There is a great deal to discover along the way.

Or to hear. It was while we were passing through a growth of small saplings of beech and maple and oak that a mysterious sound came to us with almost spine-chilling suddenness. In the beginning it was soft and low in pitch, so much so that it must have been subconsciously heard and then dismissed with an unexplained anxiety. A few moments later it came again, striking the troubled senses anew, barely but now audibly, with an overpowering force.

It did not seem like a sound at all, but rather an invisible presence, a sudden awareness of something amiss that generates chills along the spine. It resembled a soft and measured puffing, as if someone had swung a sledgehammer past our heads and missed, or as if a giant eagle had swooped down upon us quietly and zoomed away.

We froze in position. Man's instinct is to jump as if struck—to turn about sharply at such a close and intimate sound and defend himself against attack.

But there was no attacker. There was no movement except the light mountain breeze in the leaves.

We looked around. Little had changed; the morning was the same as it had been. The chestnut-sided warbler still slipped in and out among the leaf buds of the oak, as busy and nonchalant, it seemed, as before. A squirrel ran silently and obviously unconcerned along the path and disappeared around a bend of the trail. Somewhere in the forest a nuthatch could be heard, and from the distance came the full-throated song of the veery, sounding as if the bird were sliding up and down the strings of a harp. Nothing seemed to be disturbing the creatures whose home this forest was.

The "puffing" came again, as suddenly as before, but now just as suddenly came the answer to the mystery—crashing upon our consciousness like a wave on a sea wall.

We were listening to the drumming of a ruffed grouse.

The force and tempo of its wingbeats rose, like muffled rapid-fire explosions, neither near nor far, but everywhere, pervading the forest. We could not tell where the sound was coming from, or even guess how far away it was. We got the sensation of being lost and isolated, in a world where sounds originated from everywhere.

Time after time, the drummer repeated himself. We looked into every nearby thicket or hiding place, moving slowly and silently. Minutes went on. We crept on one side and searched on the other side of the trail. We waited and watched, but it was no use. We never saw the bird. We never saw or heard it fly away, and as the last of its drumming filled the forest air with pressure ridges, we reckoned that it had been very close upon the trail and hidden so well that a day-long search might not have disclosed its hiding place.

Regardless of that, we had made enough of a discovery. It had been a sound familiar and thrilling, once recognized, but it was completely unexpected and particularly striking because it was so loud.

Our hike was a rousing success at that moment. To a human being this may seem like a little thing to make such a big success. But we were judging the matter on the grouse's scale of values—or the universe's —where drumming is no small thing at all.

Lazy mornings such as this were made for hiking—relaxed, free to stop, free to pause and contemplate. We sat on a ledge and scanned the far horizon with binoculars, intent on ridges and crags and dark out-crops of rock. Beneath the living mantle of these mountains was the massive, ponderous range itself, so big that on it the skin of life is but a thin and ragged overcoat.

Big and complex and old: no other words describe the Appalachian system so fully.

The Great Smoky Mountains in which we hiked were only a part of these uplifts. The principal elements of Appalachian topography to the north are the highest mountains in Maine; the White Mountains of New Hampshire; the Green Mountains of Vermont; the Berkshires of Massachusetts, Connecticut and New York; the Catskills; the ridge and valley country of Pennsylvania and Virginia; the Alleghenies; the Cumberlands; and the Blue Ridge—that great escarpment that looks out eastward over lowlands teeming with people and cities and highways.

To the south, the terminus of The Appalachian Trail on Springer Mountain, Georgia, coincides almost exactly with the southern terminus of the Blue Ridge. Trail and Ridge both begin some sixty miles by crow southeast of Chattanooga, Tennessee.

But not even the Blue Ridge, curving and separating and rejoining as it does, invokes any order within these hopelessly jumbled ranges. Going northeastward, it separates and does not come together again until Roanoke, Virginia, 600 miles away by trail. And the Blue Ridge, ripped apart, is filled with still other mountains.

On Springer Mountain, The Appalachian Trail starts on its way at a high elevation (3,782 feet) and stays up high for most of its 2,000 miles. The A.T. starts in a wilderness, too, for from the summit of Springer Mountain one sees few vestiges of the works or destruction of men. It is an auspicious beginning.

The Trail reveals these mountains as does no other port of entry or means of transit. Not even a flying belt would give you such an intimate, compelling view, for then you would be detached and taken out of the forest through which the pathway goes. Among the friendly oaks and beeches the A.T. dips into gaps and coves and gorges. It winds along crests at the headwaters of creek after creek. One forested basin follows another, dropping away to the right and left. The hiker is on top of the world.

Here in Georgia, the Trail lies within the boundary of Chattahoochee National Forest. The footway is excellent, the forest well managed, the only danger coming from hunters in autumn if you happen to be with-out a blazing-red hat.

After 76 miles, the Trail enters North Carolina and Nantahala National Forest. Were it not for the protection of Federal agencies that administer the lands through which the pathway goes, the integrity of the Trail would be more endangered than it is. Nearly half of the Trail, 866 miles, is on private land; 452 miles are on state land. The remainder, 682 miles, is on public land, chiefly under the jurisdiction of two major bureaus—the Forest Service, U. S. Department of Agriculture, and the National Park Service, Department of the Interior.

As long ago as 1938, just after the Trail was first completed, these bureaus agreed to maintain the environs in a natural condition. Enter-ing into a mutual public agreement, the agencies designated "a zone extending for a minimum width of one mile on each side of those portions of The Appalachian Trail which pass through areas under their separate jurisdiction. . . . There will be constructed no new paralleling routes for the passage of motorized transportation, and no developments which in the judgment of the administering agency are incompatible with the existence of said zone."

There were, however, some provisos. "This agreement shall not be construed to affect the location of the Blue Ridge Parkway . . . shall not prevent logging and the construction of logging roads not open to the general public where the Trail crosses areas under management for the producion of timber . . . [and] may be terminated or modified in whole or in part upon six months' advance notice in writing given by either party hereto to the other."

The agreement has generally been honored, and where abrogated by necessity, the administering agency has relocated the Trail at its own expense. All of which is at least some assurance that the route of the

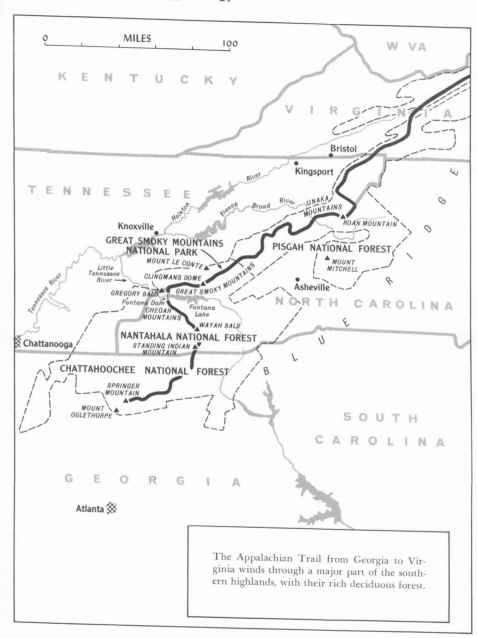

The Appalachian Trail from Georgia to Virginia winds through a major part of the southern highlands, with their rich deciduous forest.

Trail will be kept as wild as possible. Today this agreement is reinforced by the National Trails System Act of 1968, which provides for a national system of scenic and recreation trails.

In Nantahala National Forest the hiker enters a region of North Carolina mountains little known and little frequented, but one of the most interesting sections of The Appalachian Trail. "For the traveler who can make but one trip in the Southern Appalachians," says the Appalachian Trail Conference, "this will be most rewarding." And the towering landmarks that make it rewarding are Standing Indian Mountain (the "Grandstand of the Southern Appalachians") and Wayah, Wesser, and Cheoah Balds.

From the Trail there are good views into the spectacular gorge of the Nantahala River, in the land of the historic Vale of Cowee. Then up and around and over the Yellow Creek Mountains, then a downward plunge to cross Fontana Dam, and through gaps and over knobs up to Clingmans Dome in Great Smoky Mountains National Park. At Clingmans Dome, the crest of the Smokies, 6,642 feet, is reached. This is also the highest point on The Appalachian Trail—and second highest in the Appalachians.

By this time the hiker has no delusions about whether the trail is rough or whether these mountains are difficult to negotiate. "Goin' up," the mountain men would say, "you can might' nigh stand up straight and bite the ground; goin' down, a man wants hobnails in the seat of his pants."

Anxious to have the celebrated view from the Jump-off, we swung around Mount Kephart, and departed on a side trail. Here the going was much tougher, on a spur of the major trail. Across rocks and logs and beneath overhanging limbs, past beds of bluets and trailside trilliums and oxalis, we made our way.

Threading through stubborn, knee-high shrubbery, and breaking out of the trees, we came at last to a point of rocks and beyond saw nothing more than wide-open space—for a long way down.

There was hardly a sound. Hawks and swifts in the distance flew in and out among the crags without so much as a whisper of their passage crossing the gulf that separated us from them. The cliff dropped virtually sheer in a crescent whose lower slopes joined in a basin a thousand feet or more below. Brownish-gray crags that seemed to be rusted from all the rain formed a nearly naked wall around the basin, and beyond these walls spread the summits and curving ridges of the great massif.

In every direction the land lay submerged in spruce and fir and hardwoods and all but hidden from view. In a way, it seemed so simple that a single word should have sufficed to explain the origin of it all. But simple is not the word for the Appalachians. Like the Alps and Himalayas, this massif bears evidence of having been rolled and stirred and carved not once but often, perhaps continually. The mountains themselves are an end result of sculpturing and modeling processes that have been going on for millions of years. For this reason and for others, the rocks are as complex as the life that has taken root and flourished upon them. And who else but the hiker, who must pound these rocks and ridges by the hour and by the day, appreciates—or curses—them more?

Throughout the length of The Appalachian Trail, the hiker is intimately witness to a grand geologic adventure. He walks on unfamiliar kinds of porphyry. He comes upon felsite boulders in the trail. He bruises his knee on a sharp outcrop of pegmatite. He lifts his weary, sweating body over steeply rising slopes of micaceous schist, slips and skids on terraces of slate, claws across slippery slopes of granite, and struggles—heart pounding, feet dragging—over crystals of quartz and quartzite, garnet, feldspar, olivine and other rocks and minerals.

The mountain men were right. The land must have been made good and strong to hold up all those rocks.

Our attention was drawn to an exposed gray crag, almost at our elbow, where a clump of Carolina rhododendron, dwarf-flowered but exquisite, caught the afternoon sun with its petals and seemed to give off a glowing radiance of its own.

For centuries, plants like these had bloomed. For thousands of springtimes their blossoms had glistened in the sun; and for thousands of winters, despite expanding ice and searing frost, they had survived, as their forebears had survived. It would be hard to imagine the Great Smoky Mountains without their rhododendrons.

But everything begins and ends. The "everlasting" hills themselves begin and end.

In the early stages, the mountains were lifted to heights three times as high as the existing summits, pushed up slowly and inexorably over millenniums of time. In the Paleozoic Era, which started 600 million years ago, there were plains and plateaus and volcanoes, bordered or isolated by the sea. In the seas were deposited sediments, lavas, and stream-worn pebbles that would become the ingredients of the modern Appalachians.

Over what is now the eastern part of the United States a vast oceanic basin, with sprawling deltas and muddy lagoons, existed intermittently for more than 300 million years, receiving in excess of 50,000 feet of sediments.

In widespread phases of mountain-building—the birth of the Appalachians—most of these deposits were turned on edge and folded during Permian time, 270 million years ago. Once uniformly layered, these sediments were pulled and pushed by subterranean forces into a multitude of forms. Rock strata were folded down in troughs and up in domes, fractured, overturned, thrust across whole blocks of bedrock, compacted, heated to a degree so intense as to change completely their mineral structure and to create beds of an entirely different character, impregnated with supremely heated gaseous lavas that baked the rocks they touched, lifted and bent into ridges and spines, pitched and tilted into sloping domes, and jumbled into such disorder that a tenderfoot is sorely pressed to separate the Blue Ridge from the Craggies from the Blacks from the Unakas from the Plott Balsams.

Today the deposits of a vanished era have become the hardrock surfaces on which the hiker walks, and in their contorted structures he sees the unusual, sometimes bizarre, configurations of slopes and cliffs and coves. River muds have turned into shales and slates that sometimes form a natural set of stairsteps along the trail. Boulders and pebbles of

19th-century engraving of the Smokies, Mount LeConte in the background, campers in right foreground.

Ruffed grouse in the position adopted when drumming

In winter, Appalachian Trail Clubs sponsor numerous hikes. Here a hiker climbs The Trail on Glastenbury Mountain, Vermont.

PRECEDING PAGE: An abandoned cabin in the Great Smoky Mountains, evidence of another era and another world

former stream beds are now embedded in strangely patterned cliffs of conglomerate. Ocean ooze, once gathered on the floor of the ancient sea, has hardened into limestone and been lifted thousands of feet above sea level, and perhaps thrust miles away from the original site of deposition.

For 270 million years the Appalachians have been mountains more or less—high, then low, then lifted again to be beveled and tapered by time and the elements.

And during all that time there have been rivers, creeks, branches, forks and prongs at work. Some streams have slowly eroded down through overlying sediments to superimpose themselves on ridges cross-wise to their paths, cutting gaps they may still occupy (water gaps), or have abandoned (wind gaps). In New England, glaciers scraped and polished the mountains and the marks of their passing are abundant along the Trail.

Thus, slowly and inexorably, during the last few thousand millenniums, the Appalachian Mountains have assumed their present aspect: rounded, gentle, confused, upturned, rugged, pitching, and steep.

The Indians knew how steep. They affixed to this land such names as the character of the cliffs inspired. One tells how cliffs and canyons shut out all but the light of midday: Nantahala, "land of the Noonday Sun."

The old-time farmer knew how steep these mountains were. He farmed the slopes to a pitch of 50 degrees. "Many's the hill o' corn I've propped up with a rock," he claimed, "to keep it from fallin' down-hill."

The hiker also knows how steep. He needs no clinometric measurements of the angle of the slopes. He has measured their verticality with sweat and muscle power.

In fact, the steepness of the valleys and coves has served for centuries to isolate the people who occupied these mountains, and in some respects the rugged topography still isolates them. The story is heard of the hiker who saw a farmer hoeing a patch of corn deep in a mountain canyon. "Hello," the hiker called. "How do I get down there?" "Don't know," replied the farmer. "I was born here."

From places such as The Jump-off one needs almost a geologist's eye to understand and appreciate the impact of what he sees. In all their infinite variation, the geological features observed from The Appalachian Trail constitute one of the most compelling aspects of the Trail. For such a colossal show, the price of admission is small indeed.

At other times, one needs a biologist's mind and eye to understand the meaning of the environment through which the A.T. "wiggles and wingles." The hiker on The Appalachian Trail may instinctively possess a rich and enduring sympathy for this environment. A few hours' hiking in this land should give him opportunity to become poetic in outlook, to acquire almost an artist's love for the shape and form of natural features, a musician's ear for the sounds of the wilderness.

All it takes to convert a man, sometimes, is a sunrise over the mountains—or the drumming of a grouse.

A man in possession of poetic capacities will find it difficult to get very far along the Trail in a day. Some who sense the challenge of distance go twenty or thirty miles in a single day. But some find themselves so deeply compelled by the natural scene that they linger and explore while time very gently passes them by.

Or if there is an ounce of compassion in their souls, they see in the inhabitants of these mountains a kind of inspiring peace and dignity. They are drawn irresistibly by the social and psychological aspects of mountain people who came to these recesses years ago and loved the land enough to stay, or who had to stay because they could go no farther, or who were born here and never found a reason to leave.

"I went down into the valley, wunst," said one, "and I declar I nigh sultered! 'Pears like there ain't breath enough to go around, with all them people. And the water don't do a body no good; an' you cain't eat hearty, nor sleep good o' nights. Course they pay big money down thar, but I'd a heap-sight ruther ketch me a big old 'coon for his hide. Boys, I did hone for my dog Fiddler, an' the times we'd have a-huntin', and the trout fishin', an' the smell o' the woods, and nobody bossin' and jowerin' at all. I'm a hill-billy, all right, and they needn't to glory their old flat lands to me!"

Scarcely sixty years ago their society still had the peculiar characteristics of isolation. J. Russell Smith, the geographer, quotes a folklorist friend as saying in indignation, "These missionaries with their schools! I'd like to build a wall about these mountains and let the mountain people alone. *The only distinctive culture in America is here. The people live.* They sustain themselves on the meanest food. They are not interested in eating but they have time to sing ballads."

The Appalachian Trail — because it, too, is isolated — sometimes touches these people, their homes, their lives, and their farms, (or at least the rugged land they try to farm), and passes some of the most remote of their communities. Though their habits have altered with the passing generations, some of their traditions remain, and certain skills and crafts are handsomely carried on. The people may have modernized, but modernization itself is founded upon, and even includes a recreation of, the past.

Perhaps the best indication of the character of a land and its people is in the names applied to topographic and other physical features. There is a special dignity in naming. Whoever searches for something undiscovered and unnamed, and finds it, thinks first of what or whom he will immortalize by affixing the name of that person or thing to the enduring feature discovered. Names denote what is treasured in a culture, and have a peculiar way of bringing out the humor of the people.

So it is along The Appalachian Trail. The very names of side trails the hiker passes, or topographic features he strides on, or objects he sees in the course of 2,000 miles of trail are rooted in history and legend and folklore.

The A.T. is spiced with names as distinctive and homespun as Sassafras Gap, Panther Creek, Roaring Fork, Buzzards Rock, Dogtail Corners, Cranberry Pond, Music Mountain, Shady Valley, Buttermilk Falls, Devils Den, Breezy Point, and Podunk Brook. There is a point where the Blue Ridge joins the Chunky Gal Mountains. In Georgia, the Trail leads between Blood and Slaughter Mountains. Maine has Mooselookmeguntic Lake; New Jersey, a Wawayanda Mountain; and Tennessee, a Tuckaleechee Cove.

The Trail passes such places as Stink Creek, Gooch Gap, Ekaneetlee Gap, Humpback Rocks, Rocky Row Run Road, Grout Job, and Lost Spectacles Gap. You can enjoy a side trip to Potato Top, Koiner's Deadening, and Cuckoo Lookout, or take off on the Raccoon Branch Trail, the Asquamchumauke Trail, or the Skookumchuck Trail.

There is a Black Brook and a White Brook; a Straight Mountain and a Bent Arm Ridge; an Angels Rest and a Devils Pulpit.

You can look out over such features as Spy Run Gap, Nesuntabunt Mountain, Umbagog Lake, Jobildunk Ravine, and Ottauquechee Valley. If you wish to cover part of your hike with maps of the United States Geological Survey, you might choose quadrangles by the names of Noontootla and Bashbish Falls.

Devils Fork Gap lies between Big Bald and Big Butt. There are enough unprintable names to fill a booklet, and puzzling ones such as Female Pond, Surplus Pond, Fishin' Jimmy Trail, and Six Husbands Trail.

These names add the final touch to a land that literally breathes with adventures of the past. If he has even half a historian's perception and an adventurer's mind, the hiker sees in the distant valleys those hallowed grounds where men fought against the land, and then for it, then conquered it in more ways than one, and finally submitted to be conquered by it.

Down there, Daniel Boone led his men on a trail to the west. Down there, Davy Crockett was born and Matthew Fontaine Maury played as a boy before going to sea. Morgan fought down there, and Stonewall Jackson led his Confederates into the Shenandoah. Farther north it was Ethan Allen and his band of raiders in Vermont, and the Crawfords who tried to settle in the wild and primitive mountains of New Hampshire. The lands of The Appalachian Trail are the lands of Robert Frost, of Walt Whitman, of Thomas Jefferson.

With memories of men like these the hiker is never alone. One hiker, in fact, spent months on the trail with a backpack of only the barest essentials—and one of these essentials was, to him, a book by Henry David Thoreau.

We were thinking about such men on our way back from The Jump-off. As the shadows grew longer across the Trail, we hiked toward Newfound Gap.

There was a late-afternoon silence in the woods. The air was still clear, with only a trace of haze beginning to rise from the valleys below. Once in a while a swift whistled by and the voice of a distant vireo could be heard. But there was no drumming of the grouse.

The curves and contours of the mountains stood out sharply in the contrast of sunshine and shadow. In another millennium the contours would be different. The Appalachians—big and complex and old—would be lower or higher, changed as they had been changing for millions of years.

Coming up-grade, our boots scraped the dark brown rocks and soil, and the sound, repeated, grew into an almost rhythmic cadence. Our hearts pounded, and after reaching the summit of the ridge, we started down toward the gap.

Perhaps time has, in certain ways, forgotten this land. After all, what does man need of a clock when he has a good crowin' rooster? But the coming of the highway and the advent of mass communication have reduced the isolation that formerly kept these lands and their people apart from the world and often from each other. Old-timers who used to "set and think"—and sometimes jes' set—may now have succumbed to the spell of modern civilization.

If so, the mountain people of an older day may be no more. But they stamped their history, their lore and the legacy of their language and handicrafts on these mountains, and he who travels The Appalachian Trail through their terrain has time to reflect on the warmth and wonder of a passing era. If any of it lingers, it lingers longest in those remote and beautiful mountain lands reached only by trail.

3

The attention of a traveller should be particularly turned, in the first place, to the various works of Nature.

William Bartram

A Noble Forest

Scene: *The Vale of Cowee, North Carolina, May, 1776*

Enter: *William Bartram, the botanist.*

Narrator: Are you alone, sir?

Bartram: All alone in a wild Indian country, a thousand miles from my native land, and a vast distance from any settlements of white people.

N.: What about the Indians?

B.: The savage vindictive inhabitants have been lately ill-treated by the frontier Virginians, blood being spilt between them and the injury not yet wiped away by formal treaty.

N.: Then there is danger here?

B.: The Cherokees are extremely jealous of white people traveling about their mountains, especially if they should be seen peeping in amongst the rocks or digging up their earth.

N.: Is that why you are here?

B.: I am continually impelled by a restless spirit of curiosity in pursuit of new productions of nature . . . .

N.: I gather that you like it here in the wilderness?

B.: My chief happiness consists in tracing and admiring the infinite power, majesty, and perfection of the great Almighty Creator.

N.: To what purpose?

B.: I might be instrumental in discovering and introducing into my native country some original productions of nature which might become useful to society.

N.: Of all you have seen, is there any one thing that has impressed you more than others?

B. (*walking to flowering shrub*): The epithet fiery I annex to this most celebrated species of Azalea, as being expressive of the appearance of it in flower, which are in general of the colour of the finest red lead, orange and bright gold, as well as yellow and cream colour . . . .

N. (*coming over*): Have you seen a great deal of it?

B.: Clusters of the blossoms cover the shrubs in such incredible profusion on the hillsides, that suddenly opening to view from dark shades, we are alarmed with the apprehension of the hills being set on fire.

N.: The flame azalea is definitely one of your favorites, then?

B.: This is certainly the most gay and brilliant flowering shrub yet known.

The interview is imaginary, but the words are Bartram's, from his published *Travels*. Apart from the Cherokees, he was among the first to travel in these mountains alone and to appreciate the wild frontier with a naturalist's mind and eye.

Bartram—the Quaker, the dreamer, the poet. He had been a merchant and failed. He was most at home in the wild forest, hunting specimens of plants for his father's famous garden near Philadelphia, or for his correspondents in other lands. Had there been an Appalachian Trail in his day, he might have hiked its entire length; as it was, he had to find his own route through an almost trackless wilderness.

If such a project would require a good amount of self-reliance today, it must have taken a prodigious quantity then, with the added requirement of bravery. Bartram had all these in good measure. He was equally good at hunting, fishing, cooking and horsemanship. He was a good swimmer—he had to be to cross the often swollen rivers he came to. He endured both heat and cold, mosquitoes, ticks, rain, lightning—everything that renders the wilderness formidable or impenetrable to those persons unwilling to accept its terms. Bartram rarely complained. The word *hardship* had not been invented as far as he was concerned. He was attacked by all manner of creatures, from men to alligators, yet never faltered until he was attacked from within (almost blinded by scarlet fever). He loved the Indians and they him, and he talked for hours with the frontier settlers he met.

Most of all he loved the pursuit of knowledge—and the knowledge he most pursued was that about wild things. Very little escaped him. He conducted some of the earliest studies of bird migration in American history. He was the first person to discover or study or describe the Florida limpkin, Florida wolf, diamond-backed rattlesnake, four-lined chicken snake, pine snake, Florida terrapin, gopher turtle, six kinds of frogs, the oil-nut, yellow anise, yellowroot, laurel cherry, white buckeye, golden Saint Johnswort, oak-leaved hydrangea, mountain magnolia, and the famed *Franklinia*, which he and his father saved from extinction.

As for honesty and integrity, he was unimpeachable. Major John Eatton Le Conte, the Georgia botanist, followed in Bartram's footsteps years later and vouched for his reliability as an observer. "I found everything exactly as he reported it," said Le Conte.

And now, two centuries later, the noble forest still is there. Were Bartram to return to it, he would not find his old friend, "Picus principalis, the greatest crested woodpecker," which we know as the ivory-billed, or "C. migratoria, the pigeon of passage," or the "parrot of Carolina." But "the red bird, or Virginia nightingale" still sings in the forest, the wild turkey roams in the open places, and "the great meadow lark" fills the air with its song of the fields.

In fact, Bartram would happily find that a great deal remains as it was. He left a 556-page record of his own adventures and discoveries when he published, in 1791, his celebrated *Travels*, a standard measure of the original American wilderness. Some of the things that were glorious then—the musical cries of birds in the sky, the sunset through the wild oak forests, the thrilling violence of a mountain storm—are still as wonderful and compelling. Enough has been preserved for modern explorers to fancy themselves as latter-day Bartrams, taken back in fact and fancy to the rugged land of their forefathers—a refreshing and inspiring experience indeed. Enough remains for them to absorb the Bartram brand of philosophy and poetry and to behold, with rapture and astonishment as he did, the "world of mountains piled upon mountains."

In the years following Bartram's visit, the high ground of this region remained so difficult to get to that not even men with axes and saws were able to denude it all before a portion could be taken into protective custody. Of Great Smoky Mountains National Park at the time of its dedication in 1940, no fewer than 200,000 acres were virgin land.

For two centuries since the gentle Quaker botanist wandered through this forest, most of the flowering wonders of the southern highlands have survived. Although some tracts of flame azalea have been removed for one reason or another, there are still enough to grace the hills and set them afire. And in its passage along the mountain crests of Georgia, Tennessee, and North Carolina, The Appalachian Trail leads into or near some of the most beautiful natural gardens in the world.

When the sky is clear and blue, and the cool scented wind of the uplands brushes against your face—that is a special time to be in these mountains. For then the mountain flora comes to life like a ponderous engine, and the enormous annual cycle of growth once again begins. The ridges, receding in lighter shades of blue, seem almost unreal, as if painted by an artist as a backdrop for the orange of the azalea, the purple of the rhododendron, and the white and magenta of the laurel.

These three belong to a single family of plants, Ericaceae, the heaths. Bartram saw them and loved them, and the higher he went the more of them he saw. They reach their peak of development in the Appalachians, and wherever the hiker goes he is never very far from them. The mountains have become a favorable natural environment for more than twenty genera of heaths, and if there is a single abiding memory of the flora of The Appalachian Trail, from one end to the other, it is the memory of this ubiquitous family.

Blueberry graces the Trail from Georgia to Maine. Huckleberry yields delicious fruit on open spurs. Cranberry and bearberry are abundant. Indian pipe bursts out of old leaf litter like tiny fountains of snow. Low over the trail, leucothoe hangs its sprays of bell-shaped flowers. The blossoms of the sourwood, the only heath that becomes a full-fledged tree, attract great numbers of bees, and they account for the savory sourwood honey collected and sold among these hills. Sand myrtle clings to rocky ridges that are open and unprotected, where it seems as if nothing whatever could grow. Trailing arbutus survives in the wilderness reached by The Appalachian Trail, which is very fortunate indeed, because trailing arbutus has largely vanished from settled lands. All these are heaths; and other familiar members of the Ericaceae which one may encounter among these uplands are Labrador tea, pipsissewa, snowberry and wintergreen.

Perhaps they persist because they are so hardy. Heaths are to be found among tundra vegetation, in boreal forests, on deserts, along seashores and in the tropics. Such varying habitats of growth help to explain how plants so charming can be so enduring in places where wintry winds may bring temperatures down to 30 below zero.

The A.T. hiker can walk in the springtime through patches of Catawba rhododendron. The lavender flower clusters of this shrub—very often nearly of tree dimensions—thickly cover the plant. We have walked through groves that were almost pure, and so tall that the path was virtually a tunnel; we called to mind the underground galleries in potash mines where sides and ceilings glisten with crystals of red and white. Here the predominant hue is a reddish magenta; on upland meadows the rounded, flowering shrubs may even suggest the form of igloos.

In spite of the harshness of winter weather, Nature has been good to these groves. They rise head high or more, and despite the severity of climate, produce one of the greatest shows on earth. The A.T. across Roan Mountain, on the Tennessee-North Carolina border near Johnson City, Tennessee, passes a spectacular concentration of rhododendron, but the wilderness hiker sees them mile after mile in May and June.

A remarkable aerial view of mountain-top balds south of Clingmans Dome in the Great Smoky Mountains

Brilliant orange flame azalea (Rhododendron calendulaceum), one of many species of flowering shrubs that abound in the Appalachian region

PRECEDING PAGE: Joyce Kilmer National Forest, part of the Nantahala National Forest in North Carolina

Rhododendrons in bloom on one of the mysterious balds of the southern Appalachians, here on Roan Mountain in Tennessee and Georgia

Come July, the white-flowered rose-bay rhododendron, state flower of West Virginia, blooms in sheltered coves and along the steep-sided valleys of streams, shining like a torch in the shadows. The shrub itself in such protected habitats grows to thirty feet in height, which merely demonstrates that given the gentle summer, the rich and ancient soil, and the soaking rains of the Appalachians, there is hardly a plant that fails to respond by growing toward the limits of size of its species.

Yet of all the rhododendrons, none has the instant power of astonishment of the flame azalea. "Most native azaleas," says Maurice Brooks, naturalist-author of *The Appalachians*, "are judged by and compared with the flame species (*Rhododendron calendulaceum*). This is not altogether fair; a plant can be beautiful without being superlative. Flame azaleas, nevertheless, remain the standard by which other flowering shrubs, hardy in mid-latitude regions, are judged."

Lesser known among the secrets of flame azaleas is the great variation in their growth. "It is impossible to be sure how many separate species there were, or are," says Brooks. "They have crossed naturally until the genetic makeup of any individual plant is a puzzle. Plants classified as flame azaleas may be of any conceivable shade in the spectrum between palest yellow and deep brick-red. . . ."

This should come as no surprise to hikers on and off The Appalachian Trail. In the Great Smoky Mountains, west of Clingmans Dome on what is now a side trail to the A.T., we climbed some years ago to one of the prime localities for observation of the flame azalea. Through humid mists in sheltered coves, and out along steep ridges crowned with unusually luxuriant forests, we hiked to Gregory Bald, a 4,948-foot-high ridge-top meadow on the line between Tennessee and North Carolina. We must have lost a gallon of perspiration, but if the muggy heat had been twice as bad, the trip would have been worth the effort. If there were ever a Garden of Eden, it must have had a corner designed after Gregory Bald.

All around the fringes of this open meadow were shrubs of flame azalea. But natural hybridization had occurred in unusual proportions. Some of the flowers were white and some were yellow. Some were white and yellow combined. Some were salmon and pink. Others were yellow-orange and red-orange, red and deep red. A botanist of the University of Tennessee, who was also on the hike, said that he had counted on this bald no fewer than twenty-one color variations—all forms of the same species. It is now believed, however, that not one but three species are represented. In any case, William Bartram would have been thrilled if he could have seen it.

And yet, in the dazzlement of the hour, there is a curious mystery in these mountains that tends to be overlooked by the hurried visitor or the photographer focused on color. The peculiar absence of trees and shrubs on these mountain ridges commands the attention of the hiker. He is accustomed to thick forest. He walks for miles through tunnels of foliage, enclosed within the fold of vegetation that covers these mountains so richly.

Thus when he comes to open ground, as here at Gregory Bald, he can hardly believe his eyes. He is not at tree line—yonder ahead and higher he sees a continuation of the rich vegetation. Here at Gregory Bald there is a profusion of shrubs all around, but the top of the ridge is clear and uncluttered, opening to him extraordinary views of the lowlands in almost every direction.

This case of the empty summits is perhaps a mystery of little consequence to the highway traveler. But to the lover of wilderness who, like Bartram, is impelled by restless curiosity, it may become an all-consuming puzzle, especially as he hikes across one bald after another (there are eighty or more between Virginia and Georgia), each as inexplicable as the other.

Instinctively, the hiker looks for remnants of farm buildings because these balds resemble that type of "overgrown clearing," but there aren't any. Early settlers knew of Gregory Bald, however; it was here when they arrived, and for many years they grazed sheep upon it. The Cherokee Indians called it *tsistuyi*, the rabbit place, where the chief of the rabbits ruled.

The question is, in a region with more than 130 species of trees, of which some two dozen individuals reach record dimensions, where poplars and hemlocks thrive, and where on the highest slopes spreads a rich assembly of spruce and fir, why are there any open spaces? If the Appalachian balds are not man-made, as apparently they are not, what then?

Tree line lies theoretically above 7,000 feet at this latitude, but no peak in the southern Appalachians attains that height, so there ought to be no mountains devoid of forest for purely climatic reasons.

Bartram, like other early explorers, made no mention of this situation, probably because the greater part of his travels were along less mountainous routes. Yet the balds are there, curious and conspicuous. They vary in size from a quarter acre to 100 acres, with the exception of Roan Mountain Bald, which has been enlarged by man in modern times to about a thousand acres. They are not completely barren; heath balds support a tangle of shrubs, and grass balds a carpet of grass. On Andrews Bald, in the Great Smokies, is a bog where sundews grow. Natural animal communities have developed. But the balds appear naked because they contrast sharply with the forests along their fringes.

Balds exist impartially over rocks of numerous kinds—igneous, sedimentary, and metamorphic. The soil is so deep, so black, and so homogeneous that it is likely to antedate historic times, perhaps even Indian times. Adjacent to the balds grow trees of considerable antiquity whose eccentric growth rings show that they have been standing on the weather-beaten edges of these montane meadows for more than a century.

Balds have a place in Indian legend. Cherokees called them udawagunta and believed that in ancient days they were occupied by a hornet-like monster that swooped down from the heights, scooped up children, and vanished swiftly. Defenses and subterfuges against this monster, or ulagu, as it was called, never seemed to succeed, and the depredations increased. At last the creature was traced to a distant cavern on a sheer mountain slope. In desperation, the people convened a council and begged the Great Spirit for help. He was pleased to have been asked, and promptly sent a lightning stroke that sheared off the side of the mountain.

There lay the *ulagu*, stunned. The Indians attacked with spear and ax and soon put an end to it. The Great Spirit then decreed that the summits would remain unforested so that the people could station sentinels to keep lookout for other *ulagus*.

Perhaps in our time an *ulagu*, along with various unidentified flying objects, will be sighted, and the devotees of the Cherokee theory will gain in strength. In the meantime, botanical science has yet to produce a thoroughly successful explanation. Could the balds be simply burned-over areas? Perhaps—but if fire were solely at fault, there ought to be more balds than there are today. Windthrow is evident on a number of balds, and gall wasps kill oaks by the thousand; could the vegetation have been destroyed by heavy winds or rampant disease?

As the hiker treks across them, he may be entirely unaware of the mystery that has risen in an almost legendary fashion around the Appalachian balds. There is little help in seeking to explain the mysteries of balds in other places. Balds exist in Nevada where shrubby and herbaceous areas lie lower than forests of limber and bristlecone pine (there are more than a dozen "Bald Mountains" and "Bald Peaks" in Nevada). Tundra grasslands happen to exist below tree line in Wyoming's Medicine Bow Range. On the South Island of New Zealand, grasslands occupy the summits and upper slopes of the Maungatua Range, and the grass there, called *Danthonia*, is closely related to the dominant Appalachian species.

Scientists still hike to the balds in search of a solution to this seemingly simple phenomenon. They are tending now to think that the balds are bare of trees because there have been no seeds to reforest them. In the wake of the last glacial epoch there existed a warming period that nearly eliminated spruce and fir from the lower summits of the southern Appalachians. When the climate cooled again, spruce did not recover on these summits because of the absence of a nearby source of seeds. Severe attacks by wind and ice and insects have probably hindered recovery, too.

But these are theories, and the balds remain as enigmatic as when the *ulagus* surveyed the southern highlands. The hiker who scans the uplands from these open summits enjoys a major benefit of The Appalachian Trail—access and viewpoints unparalleled in the heart of a wilderness of extraordinary beauty and mystery. And at Gregory Bald, the rabbit place, he may think of these balds, blazing with flowers in June, as floral epaulets on the shoulders of the mountains.

But their beauty is a fragile beauty. Within the national parks and forests, these wild and natural gardens are reasonably protected; but even here, danger approaches: we pause on a high point of The Appalachian Trail and our gaze goes from freshly glistening banks of rhododendrons and flame azaleas down across the forested ridges, over pinnacles and into hollows where the haze of the valley hangs. Beyond the river, we see the smoke of industry seeping through the trees and among the shrubs, pushing a layer of haze and acid into the forest, filling the coves, crowding closer against the upland ridges. . . .

Narrator: And did you go on?

Bartram: I continued my lonesome pilgrimage. My road for a considerable time led me winding and turning about the steep rocky hills; the descent of some of which was very rough and troublesome, by means of fragments of rocks, slippery clay and talc; but after this I entered a spacious forest, the land having gradually acquired a more level surface; a pretty grassy vale appears on my right, through which my wandering path led me, close by the banks of a delightful creek.

N.: Altogether in your travels, what did you think of this country?

B.: I beheld with rapture and astonishment a sublimely awful scene of power and magnificence, a world of mountains piled upon mountains.

4

My plan was simply to push on in a general southward direction by the wildest, leafiest, and least trodden way I could find, promising the greatest extent of virgin forest.

John Muir

The Adventurers

There have probably always been trails of some sort on the land surface of what is now North America. Some made by prehistoric animals were probably followed by deer, buffalo, and other animals, and these in turn by the earliest Indians.

European explorers remained in debt to narrow Indian trails for dependable access to the wilderness. Rivers were sometimes unreliable—the water too high or too low, or the surface choked with ice or debris—and rivers did not always go where the explorers wanted to go. On the contrary, Indian trails, like buffalo trails, often existed in dry places where the walking was best.

Ridges, for example. If more rain fell there than in the valleys, it also ran off more quickly. Wind-blown mountain crests were often free of snow in winter, and of leaves and undergrowth at other times of the year. This meant less wear and tear on clothing. A warrior could walk silently on the ridges, and see more land around him, including the distant signs of enemies.

Indian trails were sometimes hardly trails at all. Some were narrow runways through the woods, and others less than that. The Indians shunned such things as blazes; that was a white man's innovation. Making them would have caused delay. The Indian relied upon more subtle guideposts: a broken branch, a scarcely visible footprint, a familiar grove of trees, even the stars.

If you were an Indian, you worried very little about trail maintenance. You built no bridges. You had no conveniently placed log lean-tos. You skirted obstructions, or crawled over them, or fought your way through. You simply left no sign of passage.

The Indian often traveled on hands and knees—out of sheer necessity. And woe unto him who knew not the weather, or sites of bogs and river crossings. These could mean delay, and delay could mean death.

The Indians had hunting paths that led from their own depleted environs to distant concentrations of animals. Their warrior paths connected them with enemies. Where portages and river paths were unavoidable, they grew into networks linking lakes and ponds. A few trails came to be deeply worn and rutted by the moccasins of many travelers. Trade trails, for example, followed routes of least resistance, and came to be lines of Indian commerce. Over them, naturally, rode the early scouts and traders from foreign lands: such trails led to water or salt licks, or to sources of food and materials for clothing.

Archeologists feel that North American Indians, in the days before the horse, traveled far more widely than is generally thought. There are authenticated cases of Indians traveling up to 2,000 miles and being gone for two months or more, on trips to visit friendly tribes. Some Plains Indians are known to have traveled equally far on warlike raids. Phenomenal speeds were not unheard of, either; the Tarahumare mail carrier from Chihuahua to Batopilas, Mexico, ran regularly more than 500 miles a week. *The Handbook of American Indians* tells of a Hopi messenger who had been known to run 120 miles in fifteen hours.

There was, in fact, a network of paths across the continent. One authority lists, for the southeastern United States alone, a total of 125 early Indian trails. The Iroquois of central New York went west to the Dakotas and south to Florida. The Great Warpath extended from the Creek country in what is now Alabama and Georgia to the Cherokee settlements of eastern Tennessee and then divided; a Chesapeake branch led off to Virginia and Pennsylvania and points north, while an Ohio branch led down the New and Kanawha Rivers to Indian settlements in Ohio and western Pennsylvania. This was not only a path for warriors. It was a route of emigration for no telling how many generations of people.

Other trails utilized by early white emigrants—the Black Fox Trail, the Old Cherokee Path to Virginia, the Catawba Trail, the Tuckaleechee and Southeastern Trail, the Unicoi Turnpike, and Rutherford's War Trace—were likewise "borrowed" from the Indian and helped to determine the social geography of the region. The Warrior Path itself lured many an emigrant from Maryland and Pennsylvania into the newly opened Kentucky and Tennessee regions about 1780. The reason was simple: here was a route through the wilderness that nobody had to fight to open. The distance from Philadelphia to the interior of Kentucky was nearly 800 miles if you went through Cumberland Gap. After the Indians came Thomas Walker, who turned off on the old Shawnee Trail and thence made his way to "Kaintuckee." After him came Daniel Boone, and with that the way was open for "publick travel."

"We start Early & git to Foart Chissel," wrote one of the chroniclers of the time, "whear we git some good loaf bread & good Whiskey."

Settlers and emigrants improved the Indian trails and blazed new ones of their own, continually hacking, felling, clearing and widening the paths. "Come to a turabel mountain that tired us almost to death to git over it," was an understandable complaint.

The hard work wasn't all: "We all pack up & started across Cumberland Gap. About 1 o'clock this day we met a great many people turned back for fear of Indians but our company goes on still with•good courage."

Ultimately the trails were widened into roads. The Common Road between Boston and Providence was opened in 1654; the Boston Post Road to New York (now U.S. 1), in 1672. Some were surfaced, a toll was charged, a pike was turned to let in traffic—and the turnpike came into being.

Braddock's Road, the Kentucky Road, the Cumberland Road, the

Old Charleston Trail, the Natchez Trace, the Mohawk Trail, the Iroquois Trail, the Connecticut Path, the Kittanning Path, Nemacolin's Path—north and south, the great trails turned into major avenues of communication and access. Some were simply paths of renown or notoriety, as the Trail of Tears followed by the Cherokees upon their removal to Oklahoma in 1838. Some connected with western systems, as for example, the Oregon, California, and Lewis & Clark Trails.

So North America has long had a history of trails through the wild and savage frontier. But then came the change. Stagecoaches, wagons and the pony express called for the making of roads—and when a road was born, a wilderness trail was lost. From the 1840's, the advent of railroads followed the routes of canals and trails and rendered them virtually obsolete. Walking, what there was of it, was never the same again.

The trails fell into disuse. Now and then a civic organization decried the abandonment of all physical signs of our glorious heritage, but the cries were muffled by the noise of construction gangs obliterating the ruts, burning the old signs, and tearing down the toll cabins and gate-keepers' cottages. All this, of course, was to provide a better way of life, with everything easier and more comfortable than before.

The wonder is that any part of the original trails remain. There are a few—a segment of the Oregon Trail at Scottsbluff, Nebraska; a few yards of the Santa Fe Trail here and there; a scrap of the Wilderness Road through Cumberland Gap. There are attempts to commemorate with auto routes such famous trails as the Benedict Arnold Trail in Maine and the Anthony Wayne Trail in Ohio. But a superhighway, or even a parkway, seems considerably removed from the original sweat and grime and tears and death that were required to cut these paths through the wilderness. About the only remaining place to commemorate and recreate the toil of the pioneers as they slogged along is on the back-country trails of today. The question is not who should want to recreate wilderness trails, but whether it is possible to do so.

Some persons may suggest that the Wilderness Road be resurrected in type, that hikers clad in hunting shirt and moccasins cross the stones and ford the streams. Or why not an annual historical pilgrimage, or a historical trail society? Original journals and diaries could help to make the dress and procedure authentic. Perhaps these are ultimate outgrowths of the establishment of The Appalachian Trail—or refinements that follow the winning of a trail today and securing it in the laws of the land.

"Trail" itself is a term that has had a peculiar romance in American history, and for that matter in world history. It denotes a rugged pathway along which rugged men and women explored a rugged land. Perhaps that is one reason the Appalachian Trail idea caught on so well. Yet curiously, a great deal of exploration has been done not on trails at all, but over the land itself, untrammeled.

Moreover, a vast amount of exploration has been accomplished not so much by companies of "explorers," often led by scouts and guides to whom the land was already known, but by individuals. De Tocqueville equates adventure with individualism, though not without contempt. Society in general has little use for the individualist, who has to all appearances removed himself from the stream of society for what could only be suspicious reasons. Society's attitude, to be sure, merely reinforces his resolve. But it would be a mistake to assume that every individualist is antisocial. He may simply want to be anonymous, and only temporarily. There is, in fact, a great deal of brotherhood in the wilderness.

Adventure, individualism, excitement—these have always been parts of man's will to do. Even in the affluence and complacency of Victorian England there were exploration and adventure in abundance, and there was a time when pedestrianism was all the rage.

It was not uncommon to hear of walks of fifty to eighty miles a day being performed for up to ten successive days. Some hikers did thirty-five miles a day for twenty successive days, and several people were known to have done a hundred miles in a single day.

It was the celebrated Captain Barclay who topped them all. He was well-to-do and anything but leisurely. He started at an early age to excel in feats of walking, and before long his endurance had become so well known that wagers of thousands of guineas were placed upon his contests. For one match, says his biographer, "he made an experimental trial in his lordship's park, and went one hundred and ten miles in nineteen hours and twenty-seven minutes. The state of the weather was extremely unfavourable, as it rained all day, and he was up to the ancles in mud. Considering every circumstance, this performance may be deemed the greatest upon record, being at the rate of upwards of one hundred and thirty-five miles in twenty-four hours. . . . He had performed long journies beyond the power of any man living, which was attributed to his great strength and bottom."

Barclay's crowning achievement was to walk a thousand miles in a thousand successive hours. This sounds deceptively simple at first, but some of his peers tried to do it and dropped by the wayside or severely injured themselves in the attempt. The point was that he had to walk one mile in each and every hour for a thousand hours, or 42 days. The feat was performed at Newmarket-heath in early June, 1809, and as he went along—24 miles a day, hour by hour, morning, noon, evening, midnight, and dawn—he was at times so severely pained that he cried out when he moved. Nevertheless, he did it, completing the walk amid thousands of spectators.

And what kind of diet were these feats performed on? If a man walked thirty-six miles to breakfast and thirty farther to dinner, what did he eat? The reply concerned more what walkers should not eat. "Vegetables," went the answer, "such as turnips, carrots, or potatoes, are never given, as they are watery, and of difficult digestion. On the same principle, fish must be avoided, and besides, they are not sufficiently nutritious. Neither butter nor cheese is allowed; the one being very indigestible, and the other apt to turn rancid on the stomach. Eggs are also forbidden, excepting the yolk taken raw in the morning. And it must be remarked, that salt, spiceries, and all kinds of seasonings, with the exception of vinegar, are prohibited . . . .

"With respect to liquors, they must be always taken cold; and home-brewed beer, old, but not bottled, is the best. A little red wine, however, may be given to those who are not fond of malt liquor; but never more than half a pint after dinner. Too much liquor swells the abdomen, and of course injures the breath. The quantity of beer, therefore, should not exceed three pints during the whole day, and it must be taken with breakfast and dinner, no supper being allowed. Water is never given alone, and ardent spirits are strictly prohibited, however diluted.

"It is an established rule to avoid liquids as much as possible, and no more liquor of any kind is allowed to be taken than what is merely requisite to quench the thirst. Milk is never allowed, as it curdles on the stomach. Soups are not used; nor is any thing liquid taken warm, but gruel or broth, to promote the operation of the physic."

Early Americans have also had inexhaustible energy, and they, too, have been individuals, pedestrians and adventurers. A case in point is called to mind when the hiker on Roan Mountain observes a brooding range of peaks to the south. Sometimes this range, the Black Mountains, is shrouded with fog, or draped with shawls of mist around its shoulders. Always it is huge, though this is not saying much in a land of hugeness. The Black Mountains are twenty-five miles from The Appalachian Trail, but their highest point, Mount Mitchell, has the kind of a story that a hiker would understand and take to heart.

Geology, the science of the earth, was Elisha Mitchell's love. In those days, back in the 1830's, oil still came from whales, and geology consisted of exploration, survey, reconnaissance and seemingly endless measurements.

Professor Mitchell, to hear his co-workers at the University of North Carolina tell it, was energetic, painstaking, and intelligent. His father was a farmer and his mother a fourth-generation descendant of John Eliot, the seventeenth century Puritan clergyman who brought Christianity to Massachusetts aborigines in their own language and became known as "The Apostle to the Indians."

While helping to organize a geological and agricultural survey of the state, Mitchell traveled throughout North Carolina. And as he traveled, his name and eminence spread. About 1830, he heard of a ridge in the western part of the state that was supposed to be higher than any peak in the eastern United States. At first, the story seemed absurd. Mount Washington, in New Hampshire, had often been climbed and it had been named after George Washington because it was considered higher than any peak in what was then known of the United States.

Mount Mitchell, eastern America's highest, as seen from the top of Roan Mountain

Camping out in a temporary lean-to, a drawing from "Virginia Illustrated" (1857) by the artist who called himself Porte Crayon ("pencil carrier")

PRECEDING PAGE: A typical clear stream in the Southern Highlands, just off The Appalachian Trail on the way to Alum Cave in the Great Smoky Mountains

Exterminated from the Appalachians a century ago, elk have been reintroduced into Virginia. This herd is near the Peaks of Otter.

Nevertheless, the curiosity of it whetted Elisha Mitchell's appetite for adventure; he would find the mountain and measure it.

He, of all people, should have known the dangers and difficulties this' involved, but if he did know them, he ignored them. In 1835, he led an excursion into the wilderness of western North Carolina, and on July 27, a serene and clear day, described the configurations of the skyline in his journal:

"Top of Yeates's knob; N.E. knob of Black bore N 46¾ E. Counting from Young's knob: one low one; one low one; two in one, the southern-most pointed; a round knob, same height; a double knob, then the highest; then a long low place with a knob in it; then a round three-knobby knob, equal to the highest, after which the ridge descends."

Next day, the party made its way to the crest of the ridge, where Mitchell climbed the tallest fir he could find and took observations.

"After consulting his barometer," a guide recalled, "he said that it was the highest point that he had found yet."

But he was not sure. He returned in 1838, and again in 1844. About that time, Thomas Clingman, a Congressman (later Senator and Confederate Brigadier-General) of North Carolina, who had often explored the peaks of the Appalachians, put forth a claim of having been the first to measure the highest point of the Black Mountains.

This was a matter of professional priority. It seemed fairly clear that Clingman had measured the highest peak, but had he done so before or after Mitchell? Clingman claimed that Mitchell had been mistaken in the mountain he measured.

In the ensuing furor, the highest peak was known as Clingman's Peak for a while, and Mitchell's name was transferred to the summit he had noted in his diary as the "round three-knobby knob, equal to the highest."

In 1856, Elisha Mitchell climbed the ridge once more, equipped with the finest instruments he could get, intent on correcting some errors of his earlier visits. And then the following year he went again, driven by a persistence, an urge of discovery that any hiker would understand.

On June 27, 1857, having completed about two weeks of work, Mitchell told his son that he was going across the mountain to a settlement on the Caney River to visit several of his previous guides. He promised to return the following Monday at noon, and so saying, departed.

When the following Monday came, the son arrived at the meeting place and waited for his father. No father came.

On Tuesday there was still no sign of the professor. Young Mitchell became uneasy, but there were, after all, many ways in which the elder Mitchell could have been delayed. No need yet to spread an alarm.

Wednesday came, and still no word. On Thursday morning, the son set out with a friend for the Caney River country. At Big Tom Wilson's house, they discovered that Mitchell had not been there at all. With that, the alarm was sounded.

Before nightfall on Friday, mountaineers from the North Fork of the Swannanoa were on their way up the ridge. Eighteen persons camped that night at the Mountain House, where Mitchell had scheduled his rendezvous with his son. As the search intensified, other inhabitants of the region dropped their tools and headed for the mountain. Rain poured steadily, and the mountain air grew chill. Clouds wrapped the ridge in fog.

Next morning, Saturday, the lead party, composed of experienced hunters, left the Mountain House and struck out for the top of the ridge. Scattering into smaller parties, they scoured the woods on the Caney River side, but by sundown had not turned up a trace of Mitchell's passage.

Another group had followed Mitchell's proposed route, striking a beeline from the top of the mountain toward the Caney River settlements. This was natural but slow, since there were no blazed trails to the settlements, and the search party had to traverse some rugged and dangerous country.

Watching for signs along this route, the party came across a trail in moss and fern, and followed it until it came to the first fork of the Caney. Beyond that, there was nothing. The party turned downstream on the assumption that Mitchell had followed the creek bed to avoid becoming lost after dark.

Over rough ground, the party followed the creek for several miles, when darkness came and they sprawled beside the stream, exhausted, to wait until morning. Other parties returned either to the Caney River settlements or to the Mountain House, weary and disappointed.

By Sunday morning the number of searchers had swelled with constant arrivals from the settlements below. The party camping in the Mountain House set off again in the thick fir and spruce woods, and worked its way slowly through the deep gorges that reached far down into the wilds of the Caney River.

All over the mountain, a sizable part of the population of Yancey and Buncombe counties set out to look for Mitchell, searching through rhododendron and laurel thickets, stunted birch and beech forests, and steep spruce-fir slopes of the high elevations. They searched the springs, streams, balds and craggy precipices of the uplands of the Blacks, but there was no sign of him.

The rain continued to fall. Thick cloudbanks poured like foam over the mountains, obscuring vision and hampering the hunt. By midafternoon the parties returned—with no sign of the doctor or his trail.

The Caney River group, which had followed what they were sure was Mitchell's trail, and had flung themselves beside the stream to rest until morning, picked up no further trace of the scientist's footsteps. They returned as the others did—without success.

Next day the search intensified. New routes were laid out and new areas designated, but once again by evening, no news had come in. The situation was rapidly becoming desperate. By this time the alarm had spread so far that people were flocking in from Asheville and other distant communities to help in the search.

Little hope remained that Mitchell was still alive, but if he had not been devoured by some wild beast or his remains otherwise obliterated, there might still be a chance of finding what was left of him. It had been two weeks since he had been seen.

On Tuesday a company of Buncombe men separated into three squads and set out on the hunt. Big Tom Wilson and his Caney River neighbors decided to strike off for a more distant route, across the highest peak and down the Cat-tail fork of the river. Wilson had led Mitchell over that route in 1844; perhaps Mitchell had tried to go that same way this time.

All at once they ran into footprints in the soft turf. Tracing the trail for a short distance they concluded that they were at last on the track. A runner was dispatched to inform the Buncombe men and tell them to hurry as fast as they could. The blast of a horn and firing of guns announced to other searchers that a discovery had been made.

The trail was followed rapidly downslope. After reaching a stream, the mountain men made their way along it a hundred yards until they came to a rushing cataract. There they saw footprints where someone had obviously tried to climb around the edge of a cliff. Then they saw moss clinging torn and frayed at the edge. . . .

Clambering down a steep precipice, they came upon Mitchell's body lying in a pool at the base of the falls. Marks on the bank showed that he had slipped about forty-five feet down the slope, then fallen fifteen feet into the pool.

Elisha Mitchell was interred at Asheville, then later moved to the summit of the mountain on which he had died. In 1888 a pyramidal monument of white bronze was erected over the grave under the direction of the University of North Carolina.

In the end, it was Professor Guyot who set the controversy in perspective. If Mitchell's name were to be permanently applied to the highest peak, he said, "it should not be on the ground that he first made known its true elevation, which he never did, nor himself ever claimed to have done; for the true height was not known before my measurement of 1854 . . . . Nor should it be on the ground of his having first visited it (though probably he did) . . . nor, at last, should it be because that peak was . . . thus named long before. . . . Dr. Mitchell has higher and better claims, which are universally and cheerfully acknowledged by all, to be forever remembered in connection with the Black Mountain . . . . [Clingman] could not possibly know when he first ascended it that anyone had visited or measured it before him, nor have any intention to do any injustice to Dr. Mitchell. . . ."

Weighing the evidence, the United States Geological Survey finally adopted the name Mount Mitchell, by which it has been known since.

Elisha Mitchell's mountain, elevation 6,684 feet (which is only twelve feet different from what he originally measured), now stands as the highest point east of the Black Hills—Mount Washington being 6,288 feet in height. In 1915, a century after Mitchell came to North Carolina, a portion of the mountain, including the summit itself, was purchased with public funds and set aside as Mount Mitchell State Park—the first State Park to be established in North Carolina. And the falls where he died are now called Mitchell Falls.

Today, a hard-surfaced road leads nearly to the summit, where the visitor will find picnic areas, shelters, refreshments, a museum and nature trails. From an observation tower reached by trail he obtains what must have compelled Elisha Mitchell: unlimited views of the Blacks, the Craggies, the Blue Ridge and the Great Smoky Mountains— the splendid vastness of the southern highlands.

To the hiker on The Appalachian Trail the Blacks may seem far away, but the spirit of adventure that drew Elisha Mitchell to them should be very familiar indeed. People love mountains for different reasons: to measure, to study, to look at, to walk among. Today's true hiker is a latter-day adventurer in the Mitchell tradition—attracted by the wilderness and the mountains, pressing forward with energy and ambition to spare—although he is a little more refined, a little more safe and comfortable, and far more aware that the wilderness around him is not going to last forever.

In a real sense, the hiker today is close to John Muir in his love of the outdoors. Muir was one of the first to walk among these mountains for the pure joy of it. Shouldering his bag and plant press, he struck out from Louisville on September 2, 1867, intending as he said to travel the wildest, leafiest, and least trodden way he could find. Attached to his belt was a notebook in which he recorded the impressions which were later published in his book, *A Thousand-Mile Walk to the Gulf*.

"There is nothing more eloquent in Nature than a mountain stream," he wrote, "and this is the first I ever saw. . . . Every tree, every flower, every ripple and eddy of this lovely stream seemed solemnly to feel the presence of the great Creator. Lingered in this sanctuary a long time thanking the Lord with all my heart for his goodness in allowing me to enter and enjoy it."

Muir's experiences in the mountains of the West, particularly the Sierra Nevada, were yet to come. Perhaps it was in the "glorious billowy mountain scenery" of the Appalachians that he confirmed what was to be his lifelong love of the mountains.

"Up the mountain on the state line," he wrote in his notebook, "the scenery is far grander than any I ever before beheld. The view extends from the Cumberland Mountains on the north far into Georgia and North Carolina to the south, an area of about five thousand square miles.

"Such an ocean of wooded, waving, swelling mountain beauty and grandeur is not to be described. Countless forest-clad hills, side by side in rows and groups, seemed to be enjoying the rich sunshine and remaining motionless only because they were so eagerly absorbing it. All were united by curves and slopes of inimitable softness and beauty."

Walking by day, and sometimes by night, staying in mountain cabins and talking with the mountain folk, or simply sleeping out under the open sky, Muir tramped southeastward. On the morning of September 21 he passed Blairsville, Georgia, and the next day wrote: "About noon I reached the last mountain summit on my way to the sea. It is called the Blue Ridge and before it lies a prospect very different from any I had passed, namely, a vast uniform expanse of dark pine woods, extending to the sea; an impressive view at any time and under any circumstances, but particularly so to one emerging from the mountains."

Fortunately, a hundred years later, it is still possible to experience almost the same things that Mitchell and Muir experienced. The hiker may not have at his disposal as much wilderness as they had and he may not have the strength and endurance of a Captain Barclay. Nevertheless, he is cast in their mold. When he shoulders his pack and pushes off up the trail he is of the same fine breed—as pure a pedestrian and adventurer—as any who ever walked the wild mountains.

5

Traveling Light

Virginia has more of The Appalachian Trail than any other state—462 miles of it—nearly all on one or another branch of the Blue Ridge. A few miles are shared with West Virginia. The mountains are less jumbled than in the southern highlands; here they straighten out and disappear in the distance. The Indians called them "the endless mountains."

For hundreds of miles the A.T. follows generally level ridge tops, curving northeastward in Maryland and Pennsylvania. The great advantage of this is that the hiker often has two views, one of the great Shenandoah Valley to the west and the other of the rolling Piedmont foothills to the east.

To hikers with a seeing eye, it is a world that changes endlessly with advancing footsteps on the trail. To us, there are two major highlights in this vast distance. One is the mountainous area northeast of Roanoke known as the Peaks of Otter, a few miles off The Appalachian Trail. In autumn, this section is a special treasure of color, brightened by hundreds of thousands of brilliant yellow tulip trees. In spring, it is a place of drifting clouds and moody landscapes touched with the soft magenta of flowering rhododendron. There is a chance of seeing elk here, too, for a wild herd is being re-established; originally elk must have roamed the whole of the Appalachians.

The Peaks of Otter attracted hikers and climbers long before there was an Appalachian Trail. Thomas Jefferson wrote about them; Robert E. Lee climbed them; thousands of hardy souls have seen the coming of dawn from their gray ramparts. In the cradle formed by Sharp Top, Flat Top, and Harkening Hill lies a pleasant valley with a small museum on the ecology of the deciduous forest, and a self-guiding trail that makes that forest meaningful.

The other special treat is a side trail to White Oak Canyon Falls, in Shenandoah National Park. Along this trail one enters what is today a rarity: a patch of giant virgin hemlock, locally known as the "Limberlost." Through vales and glens, beside the cascades of a mountain stream, the trail descends through a deciduous forest that is slowly recovering from the overcut of decades past. Images from hikes along that trail are engraved upon our memories—the softly shimmering mirror surfaces of rock-lined pools, the sunlight filtered through the yellow green of early hickory leaves, the reddish-brown remains of chestnut logs decaying into soil. The birds seem to have forgiven man his ravages of the past; the bears appear to harbor no resentment for depredations on their ancestors. Beneath the rocks live colorful salamanders; wild turkeys roam the edges of the meadows; throughout the forest young trees are rising; it is a natural world coming back to life, and the very rebirth gives hope that nature can put together a portion of what man has torn asunder.

White Oak Falls appears to be engulfed in forest, and one must descend below it and walk out on a point of rocks in order to see it all and feel the magic of its music. In the streams, as in the birds, the mountain wilderness finds a voice.

Destinations are not everything. Getting there is only half the fun, and the principle of The Appalachian Trail is the principle of an almost endless route. Where there are not waterfalls or soaring crags, or gorges or virgin forests, there is just plain trail—except that The Appalachian Trail is anything but plain and a hike along it anything but dull. There is always the excitement of not knowing what to expect.

The veteran hiker rarely takes off with the speed and dash of a long-distance runner, or goes crashing down the trail with sixty-inch strides. He may have tried this once, to his regret, and thenceforth adopted a steady and measured pace. Nor does The Appalachian Trail always permit a sustained and rapid progress. It is, as a matter of fact, a highly varied trail that may at times seem more like an obstacle course than a footpath.

In rural areas and the fringes of towns, which the Trail must pass of necessity, there are sometimes graded roads that permit a hiker to make good time. Likewise, in certain portions of national parks and forests, the Trail may follow abandoned railroad grades or lumbering tracks or old roadways, and one can walk without a great deal of obstruction. This is, however, a luxury not always available.

At the other extreme is the "footway," which in Trail parlance simply means a path that has not been improved. Where maintenance has lapsed, a hiker may also refer to this narrow passage as a "manway" because it has been cleared only enough for a man to squeeze his way through. The only step beyond this is pure wilderness where there is no trail at all. Indeed, The Appalachian Trail, in some places, is simply a connected series of blazes showing which way to go. This is in keeping with the wilderness character of the Trail, and it is well for the newcomer to understand that the A.T. is not a boulevard.

The veteran hiker, stepping nimbly but carefully, conscious of the perils of an accident miles from nowhere, negotiates some extremely difficult terrain. He sidesteps rocks throughout, often sharp-pointed ones, a delicate operation when autumn leaves obscure the contours of the trail. He watches for sandy surfaces that make skidding easy, or for protruding roots that could catch a toe and break an ankle. He clambers over logs or squeezes under them, or works his way through the thick limbs of some fallen giant of the forest.

His greatest difficulties may arise from a superabundance of water. Not that he must ford every stream—there are numerous bridges along The Appalachian Trail. It is not the water in streams that gives him the most trouble but the water on the trail and on the leaves of trees. In this climate the sky is often clouded and rain pouring. Such moisture yields the refreshment and luxuriance of growth that makes the deciduous forest wilderness so rich and delightful, but to the hiker it brings some problems.

Because the trail is so often an unworked footway, and because the vegetation grows faster than it can be kept cut away by maintenance crews, the hiker often plows through low-growing blueberry thickets or high-growing meadow grass drenched with rain or dew. These soak his trousers and shoes almost as completely as if he had walked in a river.

An ungraded trail is not designed to drain away all the water that falls upon it, and that which does not sink into the duff or earth remains where it is. Plop! goes the hiking boot mile after mile, prompting references to The Appalachian Trail as a "footbath through the wilderness." Rain likewise soaks and slickens rocks and moss and logs that lie in the way, adding a special tang of potential disaster to trail travel. Over bogs and watery meadows, through swamps, and across slick rocks near seeps and springs, the hiker resigns himself to slipping and sliding and getting wet. But if he can smile and surrender himself to the vagaries of nature, he is free to enjoy his hike to the fullest.

Or enjoy his torture, as the case may be. The Appalachian Trail is demanding, for wilderness itself is demanding. The use of it is not intended to be easy. The Trail never skirts a mountain just to make hiking easier; it goes to the top, or a least as high as possible. It is an alpine, ridge-line trail. This means a great deal of up and down, and since going up takes longer than going down, there seems to be twice as much of that. Very often the climbs are steep and severe, and in a few cases are on nearly vertical rock surfaces that require hand grips and toe holds. After a few miles of this, newcomers may consider that the Trail has lost some of the glamour and romance it was supposed to have.

The paradox is that the veteran hiker hardly regards all this as "roughing it"; in the words of Old Nessmuk, this is smoothing it. These tribulations actually combine with the beauty of the Trail and freshness of the air to produce a special kind of hiking experience that is one of the most exhilarating on earth. Alpine walks, as Stephen said, are the poetry of the pursuit. It may surprise the tenderfoot that wilderness walks mean hardship as well as pleasure, and he may find this difficult to understand. He is not alone. Thoreau never met but one or two persons in his life who he felt understood the art of walking.

The experienced hiker, accordingly, does not overplay the delights of his craft. Hiking can be grueling, dirty, and tedious work. It is work that requires time to be understood and appreciated. He cannot talk others into it; the discovery and the experience must be theirs and must be cumulative. He cannot lure them into a wilderness trap from which they may return exhausted and disgruntled. To paraphrase the miner's ninth commandment: *Thou shalt not tell thy neighbor false tales about good hiking in the mountains lest in deceiving thy neighbor, when he returneth through the snow with naught save his rifle, he presenteth thee with the contents thereof, and like a dog thou shalt fall down and die.*

Volunteer clubs of the Appalachian Trail Conference, plus Federal agencies through whose land the Trail runs, combine to maintain the Trail in good order. Responsibility for maintaining it is shared by the numerous Appalachian Trail Clubs. The Conference itself is composed of a Board of eighteen managers, three from each of the six districts into which the Trail route has been divided. The executive officer of the Conference is its chairman, who speaks for member clubs on Appalachian Trail matters; the clubs themselves take their own stands on local and national conservation and recreation issues.

Monetary expenses incurred in maintaining the Trail are contributed by club members. There is also a substantial expenditure of human energy in this operation because pruning shears, weeders, saws, paint, and other supplies or equipment often have to be backpacked for miles before the work begins. It is on such hard work that the trail crews seem to thrive. In Connecticut, there is a traditional marathon when the entire section of the Trail is patrolled on a single spring week end; teams walking in relay sweep along the Trail day and night until the job is done.

Throughout its length, The Appalachian Trail is clearcut; i.e., the encroaching vegetation cut away, as much as possible (or as much as suitable), blowdowns removed, major obstructions eliminated or the trail rerouted, bridges and shelters repaired and litter disposed of. Metal markers are replaced as needed, and the white-paint blazes (titanium oxide) renewed every year or every other year as necessary. (Cairns are often used to guide hikers where no trees exist and where visibility is sometimes limited, as during a fog.) Blue-blazed side trails, because of the sheer number and mileage of them, are less frequently patrolled, but they are included in the maintenance program of each overseeing club or agency.

The markings are not infallible, however, and many a jaunt in these wild mountains is spiced with a short period of being lost, especially if the walker takes off on a side trail where the blazes are less easy to see. More than once we have done this, and more than once have become completely lost. Partly this results from the fascination of the off-trail wilderness; it is a simple thing to get so interested in a bird that passes, or a patch of ripe raspberries or a compelling view, that the trail is momentarily forgotten. In that moment the trail is lost.

We have wandered through tangles of underbrush in search of the familiar markings. We have turned in error onto side roads that became extremely confusing in heavily logged areas. We have crawled through thickets along the edges of lakes, gouging our flesh and tearing our clothes before giving up and returning to the last known marker.

And there were times when we were following an open path that "no one could possibly stray from" and gone blithely ahead while the Trail branched off in another direction. Not that the markings failed to give ample warning: the double blaze—one on top of another—indicated that the Trail was to make an important turn that should not be overlooked. We simply failed to look in the right place at the right time. Such mundane things as blazes and directions are sometimes forgotten in the detachment of walking. Even Ulysses, in the Odyssey, said that he once saw a tree as beautiful as a woman.

While it may be that a veteran hiker who carries a compass, mirror,

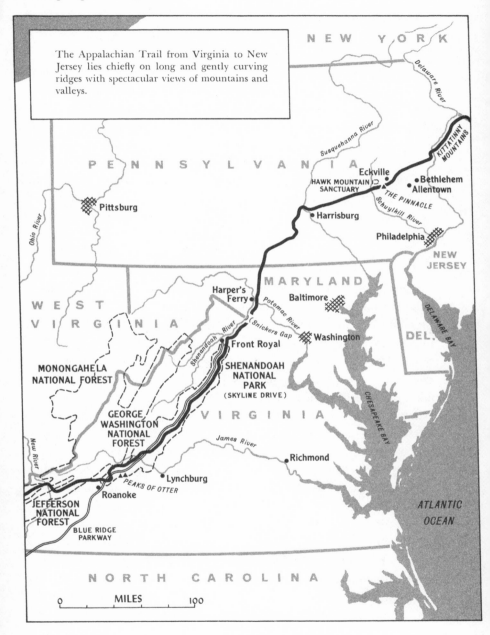

The Appalachian Trail from Virginia to New Jersey lies chiefly on long and gently curving ridges with spectacular views of mountains and valleys.

and emergency food enjoys getting lost now and then, The Appalachian Trail is not as difficult as all that, and most hikers—experienced or not —take off down the pathway without a worry.

When tired or ready for bed they stop at a conveniently located A.T. shelter. The average shelter is hardly a marble palace, but as one hiker said, there are times after a hard day's hike when a lean-to looks like the Taj Mahal. Though sometimes built of crude materials, the trailside shelter has a strictly utilitarian design. The roof is low, tapering from seven feet high in front to three feet high in back. The floor, or rather the place where sleeping gear is spread, is a bed of poles or rough planks raised about two feet from the ground; the width of the shelter determines the number of persons it can accommodate. A shelf to one side holds personal and cooking gear, and a bench in front provides additional protection as well as sitting space. There may be other benches added over a long period of time.

The design is completed by a fireplace directly in front. The fire in this position serves three functions of transcendent importance: heat for cooking, warmth when the weather is cold, and smoke to drive away insects. Lean-tos are located, wherever possible, next to a source of water, which also means that they may be located next to a source of mosquitoes. But that is a hazard of Appalachian hiking, and he who takes not insect repellent learns of his forgetfulness in an enduring way.

Some lean-tos, built more than thirty years ago by the Civilian Conservation Corps and member clubs, were well constructed and still serve, with an occasional reroofing, to protect the weary hiker.

Altogether, there are more than 225 shelters along The Appalachian Trail, ranging from handsome wood and stone buildings to the merest log lean-tos. According to plan, these shelters have been placed more or less an easy day's hike apart, and are occupied on a first-come, first-served basis—or by more than one group of hikers if there is room. Some shelters, built of saw lumber, are wooden floored, open in front, and fitted with long overhanging eaves to keep out most of the water. In the White Mountains there are the splendid "huts" or hostels, operated as a public service by the Appalachian Mountain Club. These well-built structures, open from mid-June to mid-September, provide meals and dormitorylike sleeping quarters—for a fee, of course. There are no lean-tos on the exposed summit of Mount Washington. Anyone staying overnight should stay at the huts or at the summit lodge. The weather can change suddenly.

In addition to trailside shelters there are commercial wilderness camps in Maine at which food and lodging may be obtained for a modest fee. Throughout — though sometimes at long intervals — standard public accommodations are available where the Trail comes close to towns and highways.

Guns are never needed on the Trail. Horses are not suitable or desirable either, because much of the Trail is cleared only enough to allow a man to pass. In some places both guns and horses are prohibited. Litter is usually disposed of by being carried back out; as the saying goes, you can take it with you.

The foremost aids to walking the Trail are the Appalachian Trail Guides. Most of these are published, and all are sold, by the Appalachian Trail Conference, Box 236, Harpers Ferry, West Virginia 25425, and are composed of general information as well as detailed trail data. They cover the Trail by sections, and are so carefully prepared that no intersection, no spring, no scenic view is missed. Snatches of history and a few insights into the natural history of the land are presented, as well as tips on times of year when hiking is best, and warnings about dangers lurking along the Trail. And not only do the guides cover The Appalachian Trail in close detail, most of them also provide considerable information and data about important side trails. In addition, the Appalachian Mountain Club issues a *White Mountain Guide* which provides data on side trails and is considered a necessity for hiking off The Appalachian Trail in New Hampshire.

In short, the various guides are a key to trail pleasure for the vast bulk of hikers who want to enjoy their exercise with an adequate amount of knowledge and security.

Nor are the Trail Guides all; there are Club and Conference publications that deal with supplies, suggestions for trail users, and information about equipment for hiking, camping and mountaineering. The Appalachian Trail Conference issues a periodical called *Appalachian Trailway News*, which keeps information about the Trail up to date. The Conference publishes a booklet that gives a generalized description of The Appalachian Trail and the objectives of the Appalachian Trail Conference. Another Conference publication describes in detail the history of the Trail. A list of these and other publications is available on request to the Conference at its Harpers Ferry address.

The Appalachian Mountain Club, 5 Joy Street, Boston, Massachusetts 02108, also issues a periodical—called *Appalachia*—as well as Trail Guides and a variety of books and booklets. There is a handy, pocket-sized volume called *Mountain Flowers of New England*, and a guide to canoeing in New England. The Club also sells regional guides and general books of interest to hikers and climbers. A list of publications sold by the A.M.C. is available from the Club at its Boston address.

In addition, other clubs have their own publications, and full information can be obtained by contacting them directly—see the list of names and addresses on page 162.

While many guidebooks have excellent maps, some do not; moreover, some hikers prefer detailed maps in addition to those in books. Good maps are available from certain trail clubs, including the Appalachian Mountain Club. Topographic maps of the United States Geological Survey are some of the finest available; they are printed in several scales and contain a wealth of fine detail. They may be obtained from a variety of sources, or by writing to Map Distribution Office, U.S. Geological Survey, 1200 South Eads Street, Arlington, Virginia 22202.

Interpretation of the road and trailside takes on new dimensions when the Trail passes through national and state parks and forests, which it does for more than half of its distance. Here, not far from the Trail, are campgrounds, picnic tables, accommodations, and visitor centers. There are self-guiding trails that lead through scenes of interest both to naturalists and historians. Along the Blue Ridge Parkway, for example, are restorations of a mountain farm, old-time cabins, ordinaries (inns) and canal locks. Museums in Great Smoky Mountains and Shenandoah

National Parks tell in simple terms what the land is like and how the early pioneers made something of it. Special interests are catered to by a considerable variety of publications dealing with just about everything that has ever happened in the mountains, or that is happening now, season by season. There is no reason for an A.T. hiker to be ill-informed for long.

The A.T. is a welcome place for beginners, and getting out and hiking is in itself a splendid way of learning. The tenderfoot hiker, according to one authority, occurs in three species. One is the delicate-stomach form which carries all his food in tin cans and glass jars. His shoulders are those of a weightlifter; they have to be. The second is the business variety who moves along with his duffle in a briefcase. The third is the vacationist who drives within a few yards of a shelter, hauls out and sets up a barrier of civilization around him, and never quite realizes that nature is creeping by on the other side of the trail.

The veteran hiker, on the other hand, is easily recognizable, and newcomers can do well to watch him carefully, taking note of what he wears and what he carries. He is at ease, confident, poised. If he goes any distance at all, he follows the primary maxim of the trail: go light.

He also goes sturdy. He wears tough, light, rubber-soled boots, with gripper cleats that cling to granite like suction cups. If the boots had no good arch, he didn't buy them; whatever he puts his valuable feet into has to have sufficient support.

And since there are miles to make before dark, and perhaps many days on the Trail, he clothes those feet in two pairs of wool socks, having long ago learned the perils of nylon or cotton, and indeed of such foibles as tennis shoes. On the all-important subject of socks, Jean Stephenson, long-time Editor-in-Chief of the Appalachian Trail Conference, adds this pertinent footnote: "While two pairs of socks are the standard equipment, I am slowly gaining converts to my style, started by my father over sixty-five years ago: Three pairs—that next to the skin very light wool; then athletic type sock; then the outside one heavier (but not a heavy "boot sock"). With this combination perspiration keeps the foot moist and warm (so no blisters), the outer one takes the condensation from the boot, and the middle one insulates the two. Presto: no blisters, no cramping, and as the foot expands through use it is always comfortable."

The hiker disdains shorts and breeches most of the time, and especially during fly and mosquito periods. On hot days and rocky summits, reflected heat from smooth stone surfaces can burn exposed skin and perhaps lead to serious heat prostration. No, the veteran wants long pants if he can stand them in the heat, ordinary cotton pants, for if he goes off on what the Rodgers Rangers called a "rantomscoot," which is to wander off where there is no trail, he knows that he can use the extra protection. Of course, some hikers disagree with him and prefer short pants to long, whatever the perils.

On really cold days the hiker has to consider whether or not to wear wool. This has its disadvantages in being too hot or trapping too much moisture. "Nobody that I know," said a veteran hiker, "has ever worn wool on the trail more than once." Maybe so, says the Chairman of the Appalachian Trail Conference, "but we still recommend wool for high New England summits at least."

In practice, veteran woodsmen in the north woods and in the south carry a wool shirt. Many experienced hikers wear cotton (or silk because it dries quickly and is not clammy) but carry a wool jacket on their belts in case of cold weather or high wind. Lightweight jackets filled with down or modern synthetic materials are also very effective in keeping out cold, and they have the advantage of being light.

The veteran hiker may regard a hat as perfectly useless, preferring the benefits of the sun wherever he travels in open meadows and forests. And if he can truly take it, he scorns a raincoat as well. He has discovered that hiking in a raincoat literally forces him to stew in his own juice, whereas without it he can enjoy a delightful soaking in fresh, clean rain. In fact, when the rain begins to fall, he may consider peeling off his upper garments and rolling them into his pack, no matter whether it is a warm rain or a cool one. This is real trail refreshment; there are few better ways to get closer to nature, in all its grandeur and resuscitation. And besides, skin dries faster than clothing.

A typical shelter along The Appalachian Trail, this one in Nantahala National Forest, North Carolina

A volunteer work crew taking out summer growth

PRECEDING PAGE: *Mizpah Spring Hut on Mount Clinton in the White Mountains, maintained by the Appalachian Mountain Club. The largest shelter on the Trail, it suggests the growing enthusiasm for hiking.*

Equipment recommended by the Appalachian Mountain Club for hikers in the high altitudes of the Presidential Range. Note the compass, emergency rations, windproof parka, gloves, choice of boots for varying conditions.

The truest test of the experienced hiker is his pack. Overburdened beginners usually wear themselves out in the mountains and leave behind a trail of sweat and tears. The veteran follows the principle of lightness, and in so doing subscribes to rigorous trail discipline—which is the discipline of doing without.

His pack is selected with care. He picks a style that appeals to him—rucksack, knapsack, Bavarian pack, Adirondack basket, Yukon pack, Kelte pack—as long as it is constructed according to the doctrines of strength and lack of weight. He keeps the pack away from his back as much as possible, preferring not to have a soggy shirt all day, and may even use a contoured frame to support the load.

Inside the pack are cooking and eating gear, insect repellent, first-aid and snake-bite kits (carried in an outer pocket where they are immediately available), soap, extra clothing, paper and pencil, maps, trail guides, matches, flashlight, food, sleeping gear and other supplies and equipment. He carries such things as knife, handkerchief and notebook in his pockets, and the only thing he will permit to dangle from his neck is a camera or a pair of binoculars (perhaps both), ready for use.

He is not satisfied with his tent, but it is the best that he can get: light, waterproof, durable and inexpensive. Or, since shelters are available, he may dispense with the tent entirely.

His sleeping bag is filled with down or Dacron, enclosed in plastic and fitted with a cotton inner bag.

Altogether, these items, plus food for an eight-day trip, should weigh no more than thirty pounds. This may sound impossible, but he will allow no more, and frequently has less. After all, he is a hiker and not a beast of burden. The mark of the veteran is to have enough and not too much.

His secret lies in keeping hiking equipment and supplies as featherweight as possible. Without aluminum, for example—in cups and pots and pans and binoculars—his load would be considerably heavier.

In counting the ounces, the best place to keep weight down is in the food department. Tenderfoot collections of canned goods and jars can add up to forty pounds in food alone. Actually there is no excuse for this. With powdered, crystallized, dehydrated, and freeze-dried commodities on the market today, the hiker is spared the drudgery and tedium of transporting heavy loads of food. What's more, these new-fangled foods are savory, and what looks in the raw like a slab of slate can be turned into a sizzling sirloin steak in about the time it takes to set up the tent.

Complete dried meals are available. The hiker may start, for example, with an appetizer of tomato juice; his two-ounce packet of crystals produces six servings of entirely satisfactory quality. An equivalent amount of canned tomato juice weighs ten times as much, container and all. The catch, at least for the present, is that the tomato-juice crystals cost twice as much as their original liquid equivalent.

After that there is a tempting choice of entrees. A freeze-dried pork-chop dinner contains a packet of applesauce powder that turns into a good-tasting side dish. Two boneless, freeze-dried pork chops, each weighing a little over an ounce, burgeon into a full meat course. The chops are already cooked—a great advantage on the trail—so they need only be hydrated, browned, and seasoned to taste.

Freeze-dried Swiss-steak dinners seem practically indistinguishable from the original, and a whole steak, dried, weighs one ounce. Instant mashed potatoes are excellent. Peas may taste somewhat watery but are improved by salt and butter. Powdered gravy with dried onions turns into a fine covering for potatoes and steak. Dessert may be a compote of stewed peaches.

There are ground-beef hash, chicken chow mein, shrimp, stew, chili, and many other choices for meals, variously accompanied by side dishes of green beans, milkshakes, spinach, mushrooms, sliced bananas, and tuna fish salad—all freeze-dried. To supplement the diet and round out the variety, the hiker can obtain vitamin-rich prebaked biscuits with individual jelly packets; fruitcake bars; soup packets of many kinds; gelatin and puddings; pink-lemonade crystals, and concentrated apple juice.

Breakfast has not been left out either. Four ounces of orange or pineapple juice crystals makes four full drinks. Hot cereal, hot chocolate, and hotcakes are well known in dry form, but there are also powdered ham and eggs and powdered syrup crystals.

Two of the most helpful items, especially for lunch or for hikers on short trips, are meat bars and pemmican, which require no cooking. Meat bars, solid and compact, may be either of bacon or of jerky-style meats—chiefly beef and pork—that weigh about three ounces and are sufficient for a hungry hiker's lunch. Pemmican, in its modern form, consists of a high-calorie collection of apples, raisins and nuts. For snacks, raisins, dried peaches and candy bars do very well.

The veteran hiker may stow away some extra meat and pemmican as a safety measure in case he has to spend an unplanned evening in the wilderness. One manufacturer produces a "chow belt" that supplies emergency rations of matches, spoons, water purification tablets, tropical candy bars (nonmelting), malted milk energy tablets, instant applesauce, cream, sugar, and a multipurpose food consisting of toasted soy grits, vitamins, milk, wheat and essential nutrients.

Palates will differ, and no two persons will agree on how closely these foods approach the real thing. That is not so important, however, for on the trail all foods have a distinctive flavor anyway. These are nutritious, delicious and light. That is what counts.

The reduction of water from foods means a great deal to hikers trying to keep their packs as light as possible. There is even more help through ingenious devices that replace cooking gear: plastic water bags, plastic mixing bags, presoaped scouring pads and premoistened hand and face towels.

Of course, John Muir got along without all this, and it is still possible to do so. He lived off the land and off the inhabitants. Along The Appalachian Trail today there are selected homes where hikers are welcome, and wilderness camps are spotted along the Trail, especially in Maine. And as for living off the wilderness, there are hundreds of wild foods waiting to be made into appetizing dishes, as can be learned from such books as Fernald's *Edible Wild Plants of Eastern North America*.

But if a hiker does not mind taking advantage of modern inventions to lessen the weight of his pack, there is a great deal to be gained from the marvels of freeze-drying, plastics and lightweight metal alloys.

Free of weight on the shoulders, free of weight on the mind—these are the principles of traveling light. What better prescription for relaxation, even if the hike be rugged?

The Trail itself even seems to have a therapeutic value, as if, by touching it, by walking along it, we absorb the magic of its freedom, the freshness of its air, the inspiration of the forest rebirth. Like Antaeus, we are renewed.

One day in early spring we struck out north of Snicker's Gap, along the boundary between Virginia and West Virginia. It was like walking on a carpet. The pathway was softened by moss, by beds of last year's leaves, by needles of pine, and by rich, abundant humus that never seems to wear away. The air was redolent of wild onion. Serviceberry (Amelanchier) flowers expanded on the slender trees like bits of winter snow clinging to the limbs. Some were yellow-green, where growth was not so far advanced, but in warmer places others had opened fully and stirred the forest out of its winter grays.

There was a brilliant red there, too: the seeds of maples in crimson clusters, and fresh new oak leaves glistening like autumn foliage.

Bloodroot was budding, and May apple stood abloom in patches on the forest floor. Blueberry shrubs spilled down the slopes. The alert eye could catch jack-in-the-pulpit flowering unobtrusively in shady places.

Cat brier clutched at our trousers as we moved along. Somewhere off in the woods a whining, sputtering handsaw started up, its racket carrying long distances through the trees; or a truck on a highway geared down for a steep hill—reminders that homes and highways are not very far away.

The Trail entered a rocky region, where the path was not as soft as before. White and gray cliffs below the Trail exerted an almost over-powering temptation to explore for caves and secret caches. Here and there could be seen white veins of milky quartz in streaks beneath the lichen splotches on the rock.

Tall trunks of oaks and hickories, still leafless, rose overhead as though to form cathedral naves. But these great vaults had not a single stained-glass window—only the blue and white of a sky filled with shifting clouds. Dead snags stood pitted with small holes as if sprayed with buckshot, or gouged with giant holes as if a fusillade of cannonballs had sailed through the forest.

The sound of our feet through the leaves had a disturbing quality, but then on a carpet of moss again we walked with silent footsteps. Either way, our entry into this community of life had had its effect upon the nervous tension of the animals. We sat for a while.

There was no timing, or even time itself. We had hardly settled down when a strange lament came to our ears, an almost doleful howl from above. The winds were gently pushing against two trees that were leaning on each other. Their music was like that of a hinged door turning slowly, or the plaintive cry of a child lost in the forest, or a violin being tuned before an orchestral performance. The sound was never quite the same. We sat spellbound as these arias were played out, like some mysterious ode sung by two trees to an Appalachian spring.

Somewhere through the trees could be heard the song of a brook. Butterflies, black, black-and-white, and yellow, flew by. Towhees perched in the treetops, calling. Jays squealed, and crows sang out as they flew over. The piercing notes of an ovenbird nearby came with startling suddenness. And in the background was the soft voice of the wind through the pines.

We came, after a while, to the Devil's Racecourse, a clear stream flowing over moss-covered rocks. An old log, grandly festooned with shelf fungus, formed a natural bridge upstream, and not far away a spice-bush was breaking into yellow bloom. Ferns grew in nearly every crevice, their fiddlenecks opening with a rare display of natural grace and beauty. For additional color there were trilliums and yellow and purple violets scattered across the rocky slope. For richness there were the ubiquitous May apples.

Hardly a devil's racecourse, one would think, but rather a wild garden. Beyond it, the Trail climbed northward through dry forest along the ridge top. The woods grew less thick, opening to our eyes some enchanting views across the Piedmont country to the east, and the valley of the Shenandoah to the west.

Down there, the Shenandoah River meanders sharply northward until at last it arrives, together with The Appalachian Trail, at the Potomac River. "The passage of the Potomac through the Blue Ridge," wrote Thomas Jefferson in his *Notes on Virginia*, "is, perhaps, one of the most stupendous scenes in nature. You stand on a very high point of land. On your right comes up the Shenandoah, having ranged along the foot of the mountains an hundred miles to seek a vent. On your left approaches the Potomac, in quest of a passage also. In the moment of their junction, they rush together against the mountain, rend it asunder, and pass off to the sea."

The old village of Harpers Ferry now lies here, and the historic Chesapeake and Ohio Canal passes by on its way to Cumberland, Maryland. Once more the hiker approaches sites of fabled events, and recalls such names as John Brown, Stonewall Jackson and Robert E. Lee.

Crossing the Potomac, a wide and rock-filled river, and traveling north to the Susquehanna, we are reminded that the Appalachians are a birthplace of rivers. The A.T. crosses nearly all the major ones of the eastern United States: in addition to the two above there are the Tennessee, New, French Broad, James, Lehigh, Schuylkill, Delaware, Hudson, Housatonic, Connecticut, Androscoggin, Kennebec and Penobscot West Branch.

As we came down off the mountain that day, we were simultaneously exhausted and refreshed. It had been a wonderful day, as all days must be on The Appalachian Trail—complex, harmonious, memorable.

The veteran hiker knows what these days are like. The newcomer soon gets to know them, too, to thrill to the freshness of air and of life that surround him; and then he is no longer a novice. The spirit of the mountain catches him in its spell and it is then that he understands the State Motto of West Virginia: *Montani Semper Liberi*, "Mountaineers Are Always Free."

6

When a tree falls
there is no shade.
Lao-Tze

No Trespassing

As The Appalachian Trail goes northeastward through Pennsylvania, New Jersey and New York, it becomes increasingly clear that the "right of way" is a tenuous right indeed. It is tenuous in other states besides these, but here this wilderness trail comes closest to places that are anything but wilderness, and there is less public land to go through. The change is not only remarkable; it is stark.

There is a place on the Trail where the hiker may stand and have the following either around him or within immediate view: a highway bridge across a major river; an intersection of two U.S. routes; a gasoline station; a motel; a shopping center; a railroad and a railroad station; a private estate; and a fire house—which, if he is "lucky" enough to arrive at noon, will oblige him with a siren to announce the time of day.

If he bolts successfully from that environment, he may find himself compelled to travel on country roads replete with ramshackle houses, old tubs, shaggy piles of wood, dirty garages, smashed autos and abandoned car bodies. With "No Trespassing" signs as thick as trail blazes, he begins to wonder where the wilderness went and why the Trail so often goes along country roads instead of through wild forests. There is no other way through.

In such a situation he may begin to realize how much the Trail was established through trial and trouble.

There was a time when the southern terminus of The Appalachian Trail lay on Mount Oglethorpe, in the State of Georgia. But at the end of Amicalola Ridge the surroundings gradually became incompatible with the concept of wilderness through which the Trail was by its nature intended to run. The result was that, on recommendation of the Georgia Appalachian Trail Club, the Appalachian Trail Conference in 1958 declared that henceforth Mount Oglethorpe would not be the southern terminus of the Trail, and instead designated Springer Mountain, thirteen miles to the northeast.

The then-President of the Georgia Club explained it this way: "Since the last eleven miles of the Trail and Oglethorpe itself are private property we could do nothing but stand by through the years and watch a beautiful wilderness disintegrate into a tin can dump and chicken yard. In recent years we gave up trying to paint the familiar white blazes to guide hikers along the footway of the eleven miles, since trees were removed as fast as we blazed them. Oglethorpe and the Trail End was marked by a beautiful rustic sign with routed letters a few years ago. But Oglethorpe was accessible by road and the sign fell to target practice; it is no more. . . . It is too late to save Oglethorpe, but we can save Springer by starting now."

And so the mountain dedicated to the founder of Georgia lost its link to The Appalachian Trail.

Highways are inevitable and the Trail must cross, be crossed by, or coincide with them at frequent intervals. Fields and farmlands must be traversed (pleasant enough, to be sure, but the A.T. is intended to be a wilderness trail). Housing projects and industrial developments impinge upon the Trail, and there are constant threats of new ski areas. On the ridge tops there are radar domes as well as encampments of early-warning squadrons. There are relay transmitters, power lines and weather stations. All these may be essential to defense and human progress, but the hiker is more concerned with human sanity. About the only intrusion admissible to him is a fire lookout tower or a ranger station—official assurances that someone cares for the wilderness.

A serious threat not only to the Trail but to the peace of mind of the hiker are mountain parkways, skyline drives, ridge roads and the like. Sometimes they can be located compatibly with the Trail, but the likelihood of trail relocation is ever present. The offending agencies offer to pay for relocation, but with too much of that, the A.T. could be relocated right out of existence, something the National Trails System Act was designed to prevent.

Far away from highways the shelters and lean-tos remain in good condition, but the ratio of vandalism increases the closer such facilities are to inhabited areas. It is ironic that certain sections of the Trail most accessible to the public are least desirable. The hiker might be tempted to propose a solution of high wire fencing and admission gates; but this is not wilderness either. In any case, the hiker regards the wilderness as too precious and too fragile to die at the hands of marauders.

There is the instance of the woman whose property the Trail had crossed for many years. First came wanton destruction of rare plants in her woods. Then the privacy of her dooryard was increasingly invaded. Then general vandalism. In self-defense she was compelled to cancel permission for the Trail to cross her property.

This is the sort of situation that the Appalachian Trail Conference takes special pains to avoid. Instructions in Trail Guides are explicit when the property concerned is private. The hiker must not stray. "Access here prohibited," reads one passage. Another reads, "Opposite red barn, turn right into garage driveway, then turn left down steps behind house and go around small fish pond." And in some places there are specific warnings: "Ours is a revocable privilege which was nearly lost through a dispute a few years ago—we have been warned that if annoyed by vandalism or the assumption of unwarranted 'rights,' the privilege will be promptly withdrawn."

Uncertainties arise from these words. Perhaps the dispute has flared again. Perhaps the privilege has been withdrawn in a burst of anger.

Perhaps the hiker will receive the accustomed penalty imposed upon those who transgress—commencing with a charge of buckshot.

Vandalism, real estate construction, town dumps, gondola lifts, summit restaurants, lumbering and trucking, reservoirs, roadways, pollution of springs, army maneuvers—all these detract from the wilderness aspect of the Trail and contribute in one way or another to the necessity of repair or relocation.

Going on, the hiker finally turns a corner, leaves the road, crosses a field and discovers—of all welcome sights—a trail blaze at the edge of the woods. In a moment he is back again in familiar surroundings, "escaped to the woods," as John Muir often said on his thousand-mile walk to the Gulf.

And there are indeed some wonderful woods still left along this central portion of the Appalachians. Even as the Trail swings eastward in Pennsylvania along the Blue Mountain, and the Kittatinny in New Jersey, and heads for some of the nation's most populous sectors, a hiker is able to retain the notion that he is walking through wilderness.

Kittatinny is from the Indian word meaning "endless mountain," and so it seems as our eyes attempt to trace it into the gentle mists and haze of the distance. Geologic forces beneath the crust of the earth have rolled and compressed this land into elongated folds and ridges that, curving slightly, stretch out for miles, in contrast to the confusing peaks and crossranges of the southern highlands.

In autumn, when most other leaves have fallen, the hiker notices clusters of brilliant red maple leaves hanging on like bits of forest fire bursting out on the branches. Red leaves of blueberry litter the forest floor. Once in a while you may see a dead leaf that never completed its journey to the ground, but rather was impaled upon a twig and now blows in the wind, swaying with the motions of the tree.

The mood of the ridge-top forest grows somber at this point in the circle of seasons. There is gray in the trunks of the trees and tan in the leaves of beech. Yet there is still some green: a few ferns, some moss, several clumps of grass, tall hemlocks here and there. Mountain laurel, state flower of Pennsylvania and Connecticut, grows abundantly. And on a cool November day you may find a witch hazel modestly displaying its curled yellow flowers. Even the inanimate world adds a touch of brightness to the scene, as in the case of the glistening quartzite or the yellow hues of sandstone.

At a time when all the world thinks that the forest has gone to sleep, there is life indeed. The last of the migrant birds may be passing through. Grouse can be seen speeding through the forest with split-second dodging among the low-growing limbs and underbrush.

We stood on the lookout atop Hawk Mountain one day, feeling as if we were riding the back of a horse; the shoulders to the east were ridges from which great numbers of hawks at times flew past in scattered procession. Below, to the south, lay a broad, symmetric woody bowl called "The Kettle," and beyond, the ridges at Owls Head and the Pinnacle. The Appalachian Trail, invisible from here, passed through that basin. To the west were gap after gap in ridges that faded away like rows of slatted fences—Second Mountain, Sharp Mountain, Broad Mountain, the Pocono region—all seemingly threaded by the Little Schuylkill River.

Hawk Mountain itself is a special sort of shrine, the result of a dramatic victory over gunners who once kept guard atop these ridges and slaughtered the hawks as they passed. So superb a flyway many years ago excited the admiration of conservationists, notably Mrs. C. N. Edge, who bought the mountain after long agitation and fund-raising. Maurice Broun tells of the fight to establish Hawk Mountain Sanctuary in his book, *Hawks Aloft*.

Gunners no longer perch here, but watchers do—an entirely different breed of hunter. These people are kind and gentle when it comes to wildlife, but impassioned and relentless in their drives to prevent any more extinctions of species than there already have been. As conservationists, they sometimes seem disorganized, intent on enjoying the fruits of their preservation labors. But when the chips are down, they are surprisingly coherent and speak with one voice. This is good for birds, for parks or for trails; and woe unto the exploiter who underestimates their hold upon the public conscience.

The bird watcher, as a subspecies of the genus conservationist, is not far different from the hiker. As we watched the watchers on Hawk Mountain, and listened to their talk—they were seated on sharp rocks at the lookout and most had waited hours for a glimpse of the hawks— we had an intimate view of the breed of tomorrow's captains of conservation who are replacing the gunners of yesterday. It wasn't the kind of dialogue you would expect of conquerors. The gunners, could they have listened, would have been amused.

"I remember chartering a boat off Cape May," one of the bird watchers was saying. "We saw jaegers but it was such a quick view that I don't think I should add it to my life record, do you?"

"What are those glasses you have? Seven by thirty-fives? They're the best, I've always thought."

Silent nod. Pause.

"You know, it takes years to establish a perennial garden. Sometimes it takes years to get it established the way you really want it. Takes years of planning."

"I remember when we used to garden. We used to go fishing in all our spare time, too, but then we got our first bird feeder, and that was our downfall!"

"It's absolutely essential to have a large group of young people interested in birds and conservation in order to carry this thing into the future."

"Has anything been seen yet this morning?"

"There are supposed to be some crossbills back in the hemlocks. Did you see them?"

"The last time I was here . . ."

East through Pennsylvania, into regions of greater logging activity and encroachment, the Trail bears on. There is less solitude for this simple wilderness path in a complex, almost suburbanized land. Much of the Trail crosses land by agreement with private owners, who deserve a great deal of respect for their generous public spirit.

In New Jersey, The Appalachian Trail skirts the northern edge of

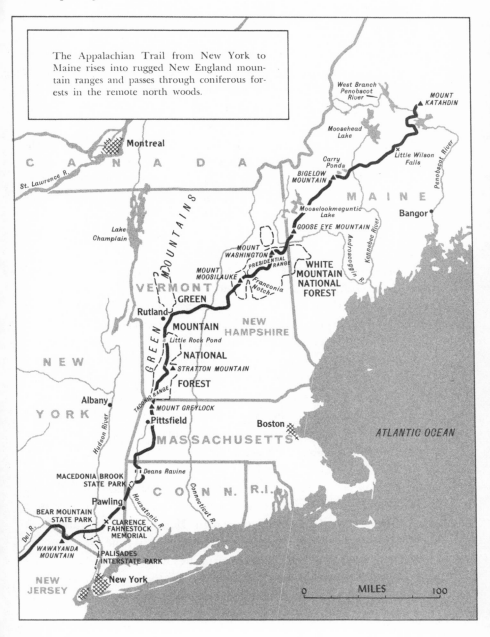

The Appalachian Trail from New York to Maine rises into rugged New England mountain ranges and passes through coniferous forests in the remote north woods.

Wawayanda Mountain, a region of low hills, rolling farm lands, placid ponds and weeping willow vales. The hiker looks down on a historic route known as the "Old Mine Road," probably the first wheeled-vehicle road in the United States, built three-hundred years or more ago by pioneer Dutch settlers to reach iron mines in the Minisink country. The road extended from Esopus (Kingston), New York, to the Delaware Water Gap.

Many of the large old homes in this region have survived from the days when Indians roamed the Delaware River Valley. These houses were sometimes used as forts in a sort of irregular line of defense. Raids, murder and kidnapings erupted up and down the Delaware Valley during the French and Indian War.

New Jersey. New York. What, if not houses crowded on houses, do these names bespeak? Is there room for a trail?

"I am actually surprised," said an Australian visitor recently, "that there are so many patches of trees in your country. In our country we picture New York, New Jersey, and Pennsylvania as simply grids of highways and power lines crowded with supermarkets and skyscrapers. I never had such a surprise as when riding through this country for the first time and seeing open farm land and even vast stretches of forest."

Forest there is, and by adroit design and careful routing, The Appalachian Trail finds a way through. Thanks to generous landowners the hiker is able to make his way across long stretches of private land that would block his way had not the trail clubs arranged for permission to cross. Fortunate, too, is the state that has such an asset as New York has in Bear Mountain—still wild, praise be.

Bear Mountain State Park lies under the jurisdiction of Palisades Interstate Park, and as such it is a veritable island of wilderness in a sea of civilization. It is contiguous with Harriman State Park, with which it joins to form the bulk of the Interstate Park. The most spectacular cliffs of diabase, rising more than five-hundred feet above the Hudson River are in the New Jersey portion of the park, and have long formed a source of beauty and inspiration, especially handy to the people of New York and other nearby cities.

Almost too handy. Before the turn of the century, the unusual hexa-gonal columns in those cliffs were being systematically blasted loose and hauled away to provide ballast for ships and stone for building con-struction. In 1899 the New Jersey Federation of Women's Clubs persuaded the Legislature to initiate action aimed at saving the cliffs and whatever was left of the once-heavy forest atop the Palisades, a forest uncut even as late as 1895. This move fell in line with the con-servation policies of Theodore Roosevelt, then Governor of New York. The two states got together in remarkable unanimity of purpose, and public funds were appropriated to start the work of safeguarding the region. But it was only a start.

George Walbridge Perkins, Chairman of the Palisades Interstate Park Commission, pointed out to the eminent banker, J. P. Morgan, that blasting across the river was reaching serious proportions and that if it persisted, a valuable scenic asset would be lost forever. Perkins was so convincing that Morgan provided a gift to stop the blasting and get the park under way.

Other gifts poured in. Edward H. Harriman, developer of railroads, had acquired a good deal of land west of Bear Mountain, forty-five miles upstream from New York City, but had died before converting any of it to public use. Mrs. Harriman in 1910 made a gift of 10,000 acres, together with a million dollars to help acquire additional parcels of land. It is interesting to note that her heirs, thirty years later, erected in the park a Jo Davidson statue of Walt Whitman in walking pose, and ordered chiseled in the granite nearby twelve lines from "The Song of the Open Road." This engraving, appropriately, is on The Appa-lachian Trail near where the Trail leaves Bear Mountain State Park and crosses the Hudson River.

In 1933 John D. Rockefeller, Jr., father of so many conservation projects, presented 700 acres that had cost nearly 10 million dollars, and included some twelve miles along the top of the Palisades in the New Jersey section of the Interstate Park.

All this, together with appropriations by the legislatures, has kept 62,301 acres more or less in its natural state—and Bear Mountain and

Harriman State Parks, both in New York, and both traversed by The Appalachian Trail, cover an area of 51,000 acres. Thus the benevolence of philanthropists and legislative assemblies, together with the hard work of men like Perkins, has made this area the contradiction that it is—a wilderness in society.

Walking up Fingerboard Mountain, near Lake Tiorati, you nearly forget that human society lies so near. This is tall oak country. In early morning, when haze and fog fill the valleys and soften the outlines of the ridges, there is a glint of moisture from every leaf, and the sun, cutting low across the treetops, seems to concentrate its rays in the beads of dew.

Flocks of blackbirds wheel about in the open spaces. Deer amble across the Trail. Squirrels and chipmunks rush about as if every day will be their last. Jays, flickers, nuthatches and crows fly in and out among the maples that mingle with oaks and hickories. Fortunately, there seems to be plenty to eat. Acorns by the million pop and bang as they fall to the rocks below, enough, it seems, to last the squirrels of Orange County a dozen years.

At times the Trail passes alternately over open granite platforms, partially clad in lichen, across spongy carpets of humus and grass, and beside cliffs partially subdued by a tenacious flora. Patches of blueberry grow among the boulders. You see on the Trail an abundance of hickory nuts half chewed and thereby know that this is a workshop and food preparation center as well as a hiking trail. You are never alone.

On either side of the Trail lie logs decaying—a situation likely to be anathema to lumbermen, but quite all right with animals currently using them for shelter or for storage bins to house the winter's supply of nuts. Actually, fallen material decays to enrich the forest floor so that some day, a century hence, perhaps (growth is slow on these mountain ridges), there will be another forest to match the one that was taken away. The heartening fact is that you now pass healthy young hickories on their slow way up to replace the ancestral giants.

The sun sends a spotlight through the leaves and illuminates a patch of singularly beautiful pegmatite crystals, composed of quartz and feldspar. The quartz has a peculiar transparency that gives it the appearance of ice permanently frozen, which is what the ancient Greeks thought it was. This simple deposit of trailside crystal is of the same stuff that went into the Abbey of St. Denis; that long has held wine for coronations; and that was once supposed to cure intoxication. Quartz is the mineral from which Nero had two goblets made and engraved with subjects from the Iliad, and in a fit of fury dashed them to pieces. Prisms of quartz for centuries have split the rays of the sun and stars into spectra. Quartz has formed lenses through which light may travel without heat. Quartz crystals have become part of radio and electronic equipment, transmitters, television, depth-sounding instruments, ballistics apparatus, periscopes, telescopes, gunsights—the list is a long one.

Here in the Trail it occurs in veins with pink feldspar crystals set in an exquisite geometric pattern. The cleavage faces of the feldspar catch the light of the sun and hurl it back with the brilliance of a reflecting diamond. One wonders at the immensity of time and pressure required to produce these minerals—and then to break up and disarrange the boulders that now lie scattered along the ridge. In one form or another, silicious minerals make up almost 90 per cent of the earth's crust, and perhaps that of the moon, Venus, Mercury and Mars as well. We are dealing with simple, but nearly universal, matter.

And so it is, in another sense, with the woods. Along the old wood roads, the dogwood turns its special brand of autumn color, so dependably and familiarly that it seems as if it must always have done so. The day is perfect for hiking, as if October, in Aldo Leopold's words, were an interlude between the other months.

The Trail steepens and the pulling grows more difficult. We rise from the valleys and break out of the forest after an arduous climb up Bear Mountain. Crossing a slab of granite we see chiseled in it: "Appalachian Trail, 13½ mi. to Arden, 1200 mi. to Vogel State Park, Ga."

The view is worth the climb, as from every summit on the Trail. The Hudson River stretches away to the southeast toward New York City, barely visible on a good day. In all directions are ridges and hills—

historic hills where the British are said to have played "Yankee Doodle" while marching past in 1777, where Fort Clinton and Fort Montgomery were stormed, where an iron furnace along Popolopen Creek was dismantled by the British to show those upstart, ragged colonists the costs of rebellion.

There are many temptations to linger as the hiker comes off the mountain and heads for the Hudson River. Nature trails, a trailside museum—one of the best in the country—swimming pools, an inn, everything for the hiker not willing or hardy enough perhaps to travel very far on the rest of the 2,000 miles of The Appalachian Trail. This is all right; perhaps only 2 per cent of any population really gets out into the wilderness and tramps through it for many miles. Suffice the other 98 per cent to come to the threshold and see from afar, or simply to know contentedly that it is there.

Besides Bear Mountain, this "midsection" of The Appalachian Trail has other decidedly scenic and interesting places, and as the hiker continues northeastward across New York and into Connecticut he finds— for all the logging and suburbia—a little wilderness still remaining, some even approaching the standards he became accustomed to down in the southern highlands.

Across the Hudson River, lowest point on the Trail and the only place where it meets tidewater or even approaches the sea, the Trail makes its way as well as possible over private lands, along wooded hills, through picturesque farming regions, and often over not altogether unpleasant gravel roads that are little frequented.

At Clarence Fahnestock Memorial State Park, in New York, lily-dappled lakes lie cupped in basins of magnificently striped granite. Such priceless parklands are reason enough to preserve some final vignettes of the American scene as it was, yet they are in reality only checkpoints, limited and artificially bound. The Appalachian Trail, as an open-end wilderness, possesses the romance of unlimited horizons that must have compelled the early trappers, mountain men, surveyors, and settlers. Parks such as Bear Mountain and Fahnestock are too few and too small to meet the present demand, much less the demand of the future.

Hikers approaching the Delaware Water Gap at the eastern extremity of The Appalachian Trail in Pennsylvania

Hawk watchers at Hawk Mountain Sanctuary, adjacent to The Appalachian Trail

PRECEDING PAGE: The Delaware Water Gap, near the point where the Trail crosses the river between Pennsylvania and New Jersey

At Bear Mountain, the Trail descends sharply (left of center) to cross the Hudson River at Bear Mountain Bridge, lowest point on the Trail's 2,000-mile length.

This is too bad, really, for there are still Pennsylvanians, New Jerseyites and New Yorkers (among others) who value the quiet dignity of a trail, who find in a tree or a stream much greater pleasure than cruising down a high-speed highway or crowding toward the seashore.

Here on the Trail there awakens in the visitor a new or renewed awareness of some reality other than the morning newspaper or the price of wheat. This reality may not be altogether easy to grasp because he may have been away from it too long, or may not have consciously known it at all. Out on the Trail he lacks the security of the local constabulary, or the hospital or even a neighbor to help in time of stress. There are opportunities for stress (broken leg, appendicitis, snake bite) but the hiker must be on his own, and besides, he is safer here than on the highway.

Loneliness itself can be a form of stress, for man is principally a colonial species, and breaking away from the colony is almost biologically wrong. An eminent psychologist, aware of both the intricacies of stress and the beauties of wilderness, once told us that whereas one man may find exhilaration on a mountaintop, another may go mad.

Of course, a colony of animals is not the same as a colony of men, and sometimes we assume that if one man must set himself apart for a quiet rest, then all must do so. This leads those of us who love the out-of-doors to speak with glibness in defense of a doctrine that we think everybody accepts. Not so. Max Beerbohm said: "I never will go out for a walk. My objection to it is that it stops the brain . . . [which] wraps itself up in its own convolutions, and falls into a dreamless slumber from which nothing can rouse it till the body has been safely deposited indoors again."

One of the fundamental, but obviously not quite universal, laws of nature is that man benefits immensely from outdoor life. Though The Appalachian Trail is decidedly not for everyone, not even here near the great metropolises that seem to need open space more than anywhere else, we like to think that such trails are for just about everyone, and that there is a little of Muir and Mitchell and Whitman in nearly all of us. We prefer to believe that a large percentage of people need to walk out in the open now and then for a few of the reasons that Trevelyan had:

"There are times when my thoughts, having been duly concentrated on the right spot, refuse to fire, and will think nothing except general misery; and such times, I suppose, are known to all of us. On these occasions my recipe is to go for a long walk. My thoughts start out with me like blood-stained mutineers debauching themselves on board the ship they have captured, but I bring them home at nightfall, larking and tumbling over each other like happy little boy-scouts at play, yet obedient to every order to 'concentrate' for any purpose."

Nothing is less akin to panic than the eternal woods, or more conducive to steadfastness than a recollection that the woods and rocks and lakes have been there for thousands of years.

When the hiker gazes into the trees that bend before the wind, when his eyes grow soft and mild before the fluttering leaves or before the flickering flames of a campfire, he acquires a new or renewed perspective of his world. With this wild-born sense of reality comes a sense of peace and freedom—the freedom of the trail. It is a personal discovery, and that is the best kind of discovery there is.

Perhaps best of all he knows now that his fellow men are beside him. Through enactment of the National Trails System Act of 1968, Congress provided for the Trail to be kept and maintained much as it is today: a low cost, high quality path watched over by citizen groups. However, if land is needed to protect the right-of-way and cannot be gotten by agreement, donation, exchange or purchase, the government may obtain the minimum required rights by condemnation.

The "Appalachian National Scenic Trail" was placed under the Administration of the Secretary of the Interior, in consultation with the Secretary of Agriculture, and with the help of an advisory council not to exceed thirty-five members. The role of private citizens still remains paramount however. And that is as it should be. The Trail is still a simple personal experience where, like Trevelyan, our thoughts may be set afire.

7

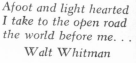

Afoot and light hearted
I take to the open road
the world before me. . . .
Walt Whitman

The Backpackers

"One pair of boots lasted the whole way, but they were in tatters at the end."

Earl Shaffer reached Katahdin on August 5, 1948, after 123 nights on the Trail, and an average seventeen miles of hiking a day since leaving the southern terminus in Georgia. He was the first man to hike the whole 2,000 miles of The Appalachian Trail in a single summer.

The human body can take a great deal of punishment. Or is it nourishment? Another hiker completed the Trail from end to end one summer, inserting hundreds of miles of side trails, for a total 146 days of hiking. All of which suggests that, in some persons at least, the body was made more for walking than for resting.

Another hiker went from north to south on the Trail in ninety-nine days, a grueling average of just over twenty miles a day, but he did not recommend this north-to-south direction of hiking; there are fewer springs running, fewer flowers and birds, and the possibility of snow at both ends of the Trail. The point is that spring went north and he went south; the more pleasing prospects are for those who go north with the spring.

Two college students, James F. Fox, Jr., and Paul A. Gerhard, hiked the Trail in 1963. "For many years," they wrote in *Appalachian Trailway News*, "both of us had had a more or less latent desire to hike the length of the Appalachian Trail. We won't go into the reasons for this; anyone who hikes will understand. . . .

"Preparations included buying all of the guides and maps and revising them according to the latest trail data. We . . . made lists of all stores we would find on or near the Trail and distances between them . . . pored through catalogues, selecting the lightest possible equipment.

"We hiked 94 days, averaging about 21¼ miles per day. (Our pace was dictated by the length of our summer vacation.) On each day we hiked between 3 and 35 miles. . . .

"Physical conditioning is but a small part of the preparation for the hike. Mental conditioning is all-important. It takes perseverance to keep hiking, day after day, rain or shine. We hiked all day every day except when we got mail. Then we would take a half day off to answer letters. . . .

"A typical day started with us waking when the sun came up or by 5:00 A.M. (EST). We got up, turned the sleeping bags inside out to dry, split the cold cereal and one quart of milk, and took a vitamin. After cleaning the dishes with paper towels, and packing, we would burn our trash and leave by 6:30.

"To get a good section of mileage out of the way before lunch, we would simply hike at a steady pace without stopping. We could depend on 2 miles per hour and occasionally made up to 4 miles per hour; 12 miles by noon was fair, 10 by 10 was good, and once we got 8 miles by 8:00 A.M. Making stops—of any length—was what cut down mileage. . . .

"Drought was a problem much of the way, especially south of Roanoke and in Pennsylvania. We soon learned to do without water, hiking as much as one entire day without a drink. At our pace it was a minor problem, for surely somewhere in 20 miles there would be some water. We stopped carrying spare water the second week.

"Upon getting to a town, either on the Trail or by going off it, we would check our stores and buy only enough food to get us to the next one. Usually this was from one to three days. We would also get a quart of fresh milk, two pints of ice cream and sandwich material; and then move out to the front porch to begin repacking things in plastic bags. By removing the useless tare, even to the extent of candy bar wrappers, we could often save over a pound of all important weight. That, we found, was the way to hike—all useless, excess weight had to go. Though we often commented that our pack weight (18–25 lbs.) was negligible, extra weight is quickly magnified after 20 miles. . . .

"Usually our lunch period would be about 45 minutes. Often we would relax with our shoes off. (Many times this was due to having to wring out wet socks.) One would spread out plastic bags of raisins, peanuts, cheese, crackers and a chocolate bar, while the other would fix the Wyler's Lemonade mix in the quart shaker. Then while eating, we would write in the log, study the maps and guide or just rest. Then onward again, maybe stopping again later for a quick lunch seven miles from where we planned to stay or at a town if we passed one. . . .

"While we could remain almost dry in the rain by using our 'poncho-tent,' it was, of necessity, minimal and we always tried for some sort of shelter if rain threatened. The sleeping bags were never too cold but often it became 'too hot to stay in and too buggy to stay out.' We had insects most of the way. At night we would switch to long pants (also for the cold) and we soon found a spray can of repellent to be worth its weight.

"Once picking a place to stay or often simply hiking till dark, we would continue on the Trail until about 7:30 at the latest. This gave us time to start the gasoline stove, cook a 2½ quart pot full of noodles or macaroni, split it, add the sauce and a can of Spam, and then lie down to a hot dinner. We would also fix a quart of powdered milk, adding some sugar to make it palatable, and a vitamin pill. If there was light, entries would be made in the log before the dishes were wiped out or washed with the brillo pad. Then we would carefully pack our spare clothes under our hips, and possibly shoulders, for padding and get to sleep. By using all our padding for our hips, we quickly found we could get a good night's sleep on a hard floor with no air mattress.

"We slept in lean-tos about fifty per cent of the time. Several rainy nights were spent under picnic tables; several in motels or hotels. We spent two nights in the A.M.C. Huts in the White Mountains and one night in the comfort station at Clingmans Dome in the Smokies. We slept in farmyards, right on the Trail, in garages, or in homes. Soon after realizing that wherever there were people tremendous hospitality and fellowship was offered to the long distance hiker, we found it a pleasure to ask if we could camp under someone's porch should it rain. This always rewarded us with an evening of fellowship, new friends and sometimes food, thus becoming an important factor in our journey. . . .

"We saw a great deal of wildlife, but not as much as would have been seen on a slower trip. We saw bear, deer, moose, many grouse, one rattlesnake and many non-poisonous snakes, farm dogs and many other species. Once, in Pennsylvania, we saw eight deer before breakfast. One bear gave us some trouble. It was a tame bear that had just been turned loose in the woods, was hungry and was not afraid of people. . . . We retreated to a nearby firetower where we spent the night. . . .

"We were generally in good health, although each lost about 10 pounds during the hike. . . . Against everyone's advice, we wore short pants for most of the trip and are glad that we did. We preferred the sting of nettles and the cut of briars to the sweat of long pants. The cushion-foot socks were very comfortable and wore very well, although they didn't last for the one-year guarantee."

Fox and Gerhard were young, but the urge and ability to hike The Appalachian Trail has nothing to do with age. Their feat was exceeded earlier by someone much older—and by a woman at that.

Her name was Emma Gatewood, though she came to be known as Grandma Gatewood to those who saw her on the Trail. She was the mother of eleven and grandmother of twenty-three. In 1955, at the age of sixty-seven, she hiked the length of The Appalachian Trail in 146 days. And that was only the beginning.

From all reports, everything was against her. She was apparently ill prepared. Her feet swelled in size from 8½ to 10. The solitude seemed to oppress rather than buoy her and she sometimes left the Trail to find a house and someone to talk to. She does not even seem to have gotten pleasure out of the flowers, the woods or the sunsets.

But there was something about the Trail that she liked, for two years later she hiked it again, end to end, this time in 142 days. In the years that followed she returned to the Trail whenever she could. In 1963, at close to seventy-five years of age, she started on May 6 near the Susquehanna River in Pennsylvania and hiked 900 miles to Deep Gap near the North Carolina-Georgia border, finishing the trip early in August for an average fourteen miles a day.

In 1968 a Missouri metal-finisher named Elmer Onstott hiked the entire Trail alone in his 70th year. A vegetarian, he lived primarily on nuts and raisins while hiking. Most needed to complete the trip, he said, were desire, time, stamina and perseverance.

Why do they go all the way, these "long trailers," and what do they get out of it?

"I think that making this hike meant more to me than anything I have ever done," said Eugene Espy, a twenty-four-year-old Georgia engineer who was second to hike the full length in a single season.

"To satisfy an old wanderlust feeling," said another long trailer, "to do something different from my usual routine. What I got out of it was the sport and more relaxation than I ever had before."

These hikes are spectacular and fascinating, yet most persons, even if they wished to, have neither time nor capability for going so far so quickly. For the average hiker, trips must be shorter, but not necessarily less impressive; and short-distance hikers also have their reasons and remembrances.

A fifty-five-year-old Ohio housewife, after hiking for two weeks with her daughter, said, "I can recall every minute detail of the trip, especially the moccasin flowers and oxalis, a mother partridge limping and fluttering away, the salamanders and porcupines, the native trout we caught and ate, the sun and the rain and the storms; all wonderful. My only regret is that I live so far from the Trail that I cannot avail myself of the precious privilege as often as I would like."

What stimulates this attitude, and why is it so strong? Why do people hike in the first place? There is no more reason for answering these questions than for answering such questions as why people fish or go to a ball game, or attend a concert; yet there are benefits and insights to be gained by an analysis of the hiker's motives, and because he is sometimes misunderstood, so is his battle to preserve the wilderness.

First and foremost, a majority of people hike because they get a great deal of pleasure out of doing so. They hike for the sheer fun of it, or as the Appalachian Mountain Club has so long said, "it's fun to climb." Fun it is, and such a satisfying pastime is its own reward.

Jean Stephenson, Editor-in-Chief of the Appalachian Trail Conference, tells this story about a group of hikers in Washington, D.C.:

"Years ago when the local club here used to board the chartered bus behind the Treasury, an older woman friend called me to ask if I would invite a young girl who was here working for a Congressman to accompany us some day. I did so, and she joined the club and went out regularly. I finally asked her why, when she had never walked before, she suddenly decided to do so. She said that everyone she knew walked up and down F Street or drove aimlessly around to get the air, or went to a movie or a dance and either acted bored or else got hectically excited, but never seemed to really enjoy anything! And then she had noticed our crowd; in the morning all were eager to go and obviously anticipated a good time, and returned at night, dirty, obviously weary, sometimes stiff and yet bubbling over with pleasure like children having a wonderful time; and she wanted to meet some people who, for one day at least, could be natural and enjoy life!"

For many people, the idea of hiking—indeed, the principle on which The Appalachian Trail was founded—is to get away from the cares of civilization.

Everything changes: change of scene and sounds, change of pace, change of touch. Artificial noise and vibration are replaced by quiet or by less nerve-racking sounds. The hiker feels the good clean soil beneath his feet, and walks on a rough trail rather than a carpeted floor. He feels and smells the scented wind of the mountains instead of refrigerated air from a cabinet. He may even enjoy a change of taste. Up here, if he wishes, he can chew on bark or resin, crunch on a straw all day, or refresh his palate at a mountain brook. If there are problems here, they are different problems.

Elmer C. Adams, a Detroit columnist and philosopher, once took a hike alone on the Trail in the Great Smokies "to cast loose from the work and worries of home. In the fulfillment of that desire, by release that was quick and, for the duration of my stay, nearly absolute, no vacation has ever excelled this one on The Appalachian Trail. One good and sufficient reason was that I simply had no leisure to dwell upon the affairs of home. Too many affairs of a different character engrossed me there in the mountains."

This is a world of the thinker and wonderer. It is a world that the poet rejoices in, and few have had the insight of Helen Frazee-Bower:

> Trails are not dust and pebbles on a hill,
> Nor even grass and wild buds by a lake;
> Trails are adventure and a hand to still
> The restless pulse of life when men would break
> Their minds with weight of thinking. Trails are peace,
> The call to dreams, the challenge to ascent;
> Trails are the brisk unfolding of release
> From bitterness and from discouragement.
> Trails are the random writing on the wall
> That tells how every man, grown tired at heart
> Of things correct and ordered, comes to scrawl
> His happy hour down—then goes to start
> Life over with new eagerness and zest.
> Who builds a trail finds labor that is rest!

Some reasons for hiking are simple: exploration, curiosity, enjoyment, education, challenge, adventure, solitude, inspiration, ambition, recreation, photography, bird watching, a family outing, to name a few. Others are not so easy to define.

Could it be, as science suggests, that there are primary drives ("tissue conditions") that force a man into search for air, activity or rest? Perhaps these are so basic as to be obvious. If so, then are there secondary drives which are equally or more revealing, and more complex?

One motive, say researchers, may be the satisfaction of doing things in the wilderness that would be socially unacceptable at home, that is, almost a socially acceptable reversion to childhood. The hiker can go without combing his hair or shaving and will be accepted as perfectly normal. He can get dirty and his friends will still speak to him jovially. His clothes may be in tatters, and people think nothing of it. If there happens to be a little rock dust on his shirt or trousers, or if his clothes are a trifle torn, so much the better. Of such stuff are hiking heroes made. The hiker doesn't have to talk very much, say witty things, hold a glass in his hands, or laugh lightly at banalities. His is a world of opposites, and no one cares or worries about it.

He can shout if he wishes or sing a tune in any key, and the only scolds he gets are from the jays and crows above. He is his own boss, free as the birds and the wind. That, indeed, is the whole idea. He is emancipated.

Kipling, in his essay on "Independence" speaks of the age-old need of man to get away from his tribe for a while, to be by himself.

The hiker, in effect, flees from protocol. There is no social hierarchy among the trees. The best relaxation, it has been said, comes not from doing nothing, but from doing entirely different things.

The desire to be different may play a subconscious role among family hikers, too. For a husband, the trail environment offers a chance to prove his skills and prowess in a rugged outdoor world. He can be "master of the house" in a way that might not be prudent at home!

For the wife, such an arrangement has distinct advantages. While camping, she may get more help from her husband than she normally would at home; there he is preoccupied with his job; here he helps with tasks that he is assumed to be more proficient at: cutting wood, kindling fires, and spreading out sleeping bags. He may even be skilled in outdoor cookery and that, for her, is a welcome change indeed.

Whatever regimentation the hiker has suffered, at work or at home, his aversions to it vanish or are subdued in the wilderness. The trail is a symbol of release.

"Something exciting is going on outside," said Elmer Adams, speaking of days when he had to stay in the city, "something vitally allied to the affairs of the living, breathing universe, and I, housed up within my plaster walls, am shamefully missing it."

Out here, also, there is security. Here are the dependable, even predictable, actions of wind, storms, plants and animals. Here are the basic life processes that man, the biological species, was founded upon and grew up on. His whole physical and psychological structure has been adapted to living in nature, so the hiker may feel a special exhilaration in returning to this basic natural environment. He may even have an esthetic appreciation of the harmony of the wild, and a new sense of self-reliance.

"Some of us hike because it's habit-forming and we're caught up in it," Stanley A. Murray, Chairman of the Appalachian Trail Conference, once told us. "It gets in our blood. Maybe it holds life in a better balance."

In pursuit of such a balance, some hikers may approach a kind of outdoor puritanism, and look at their trail experiences in a strictly spartan way. They may endure the treacherous dangers of freezing rain, slippery rocks, icy clothes, ice-filled wind and blinding fog, which test the limits of endurance, exhaustion and self-denial. It is almost a rite of self-purification, or of "purging the physic," reminiscent of Captain Barclay's days of pedestrianism. Discipline is a strictly human trait.

On the other hand, nondiscipline is a form of leisure, too—the ability to "stretch out" physically and mentally. Hans Zbinden, in the *American-German Review*, points out that rehabilitation of human beings is a subject of increasing concern to European and American sociologists, but that little success can be expected in an environment where there is a frenetic state of activity. His recipe for rehabilitation is simple. "A weekend devoted to achieving the most difficult but satisfying state of all: glorious, abundant idleness, wanting nothing more than to dream and muse, to relish the joy of being alive and of savoring little, unimportant things . . . . this would be considered by the hustlers to be a thoroughly wasted weekend."

Why hike? There may be hundreds of personal, sentimental reasons for getting out on the trail: lonely persons wanting companionship, college athletes preparing for track, scouts earning merit badges, overweight people trying to reduce, devotees of the wilderness, researchers, writers, artists, dreamers, explorers, sightseers, philosophers, the poor, the rich, the sick. No wonder so many people join in the public defense of trails and wilderness.

Not least of the lures of hiking is plain and simple exercise. Galen, a second-century Greek physician, wrote in his *Code of Health* that "exercise, by promoting at once absorption and secretion, promotes life without hurrying it, renovates all the parts, and preserves them apt and fit for every office."

And which exercise is best? Thomas Jefferson left no doubt about his feelings on the matter. "Walking is the best possible exercise," he said. "Habituate yourself to walk very far. The Europeans value themselves on having subdued the horse to the uses of man; but I doubt whether we have not lost more than we have gained, by the use of this animal."

There is something in The Appalachian Trail for almost everyone, whether he hikes a day or a summer. And although there has been no survey that we know of to prove or disprove it, the hiker probably comes back with more than he started out in search of. He is not unlike the legendary Princes of Serendip (Ceylon) who on their voyages found better things than what they sought, and after whom Walpole coined the word "serendipity."

Perhaps the hiker has met new friends. Perhaps the open air has been a stimulus to his jaded imagination. Perhaps he has had new experiences and from them generated new ideas. He can devise a spiritual, moral and physical code of his own—if he thinks he needs one. Here, if anywhere, he can be a full-fledged romanticist; conversely, as a pragmatist, he can reorganize his life into a more meaningful pattern.

The Appalachian Trail is one of the last strongholds of peace in a congested and largely urban part of the world. Along it the hiker finds elbowroom and silence. And when he is bruised and battered, wind-blown, disciplined—and finally reorganized—then, of all things, it is nice to get home.

Just before leaving New York state, The Appalachian Trail passes a reserved area supervised by the Nature Conservancy, an organization dedicated to saving some of the nation's green spaces before they are all absorbed by the growth of suburbia. This one, near Pawling, was established in 1959. Regulations prohibit hunting, entry of pets, or any disturbance of the natural scene. Here, therefore, the hiker can study plants and animals in 1,000 acres of wild habitat during the year's four seasons. Well-marked trails lead through the sanctuary and past some steep, spectacular ravines.

On the other side of the line, the Trail winds through Macedonia Brook State Park, Connecticut, with pleasant streams and a superb stand of hardwoods, offering fine avenues for quiet walking. State parks, like national parks, give sanctuary to parts of The Appalachian Trail, and to animals and plants as well. Here the hiker is likely to observe deer and grouse with which the forest abounds.

The Housatonic River, sometimes a wide and placid waterway, some-times a narrow one full of rapids, is overhung by oaks and maples, and its ponds have no doubt for centuries been a haven for ducks.

Between Kent and Macedonia are splendid views of the Housatonic, plus a mile or so of the old Albany Post Road, recalling the romance of a bygone era. The road is hollowed out, steep, and narrow, with stone walls on either side sinking into the earth, enormous trees, and wild-grape vines the thickness of a forearm. The upland fields have changed little, and it is easy to imagine the stagecoaches skidding down this hill on the road to Albany.

Along the Housatonic, one feels the special beauty and tranquility of the Connecticut countryside. We are not far from civilization here; indeed, we are surrounded by it. But we seem set apart, as if the estates, the farms and the quiet villages were far away. This impression is heightened even more when we descend into a place as charming and unforgettable as Deans Ravine.

We need no sunlight to savor the softness and beauty of this wooded dell. Deans Ravine is the kind of place you can get to know and appreciate in shade and rain, and for all we know, in snow. It is buried in forest, and though scarcely a mile long, it is a miracle mile in its own quiet way. The hiker enters the ravine as if sinking into an ocean of trees, down through groves of hemlock, whose many-branched trunks reach almost twenty feet in circumference. Stately they stand on the uneven floor of the depression. The rock and soil are rich with hemlock needles, an accumulation of decades, and the leaves of maple, hickory, beech and witch hazel. We walk past violets and yellow mushrooms, and beside gray rocks and trees that are moss- and lichen-covered. Among them grow an unusual variety of ferns: Christmas, bracken, maidenhair, and others less easy to identify. The Appalachians are full of ferns, wherever you go, on dry slopes or wet. A great variety of them may be seen, and the hiker on The Appalachian Trail is never very far from a cool, green patch of them.

Here the clumps of fern extend down to the edge of the stream, where asters and goldenrods grow, and wild grape forms thickets. We find the familiar gray and white bark of the sycamore, plus the birch, both water-loving and adding a light touch to the shadows of the forest. Chickadees chatter in the trees, and white-breasted nuthatches move up and down the hemlock trunks.

Yellow touch-me-nots, set in thick clusters by the water's edge, seem perfectly arranged, as if by a master florist. Here and there stand cardinal flowers, bright spots of red in the gloom. Jack-in-the-pulpits lie low beneath the trees, their color delicate and complementary to the scene. Even the poison ivy, with handsome glistening leaves, is not to be deprecated in this natural garden.

At the head of the ravine, we come to a picturesque waterfall, festooned with banks of touch-me-not. Layers of rock, broken off in

The Pennine Way, England's long-distance trail across the top of the Pennines, crosses Crag Lough (right) in Northumberland National Park.

The Pacific Crest trail system covers such spectacular mountain scenery as these Sierra peaks in California.

On the summit of Mount Greylock in Western Massachusetts, such rare birds as Bicknell's Thrush must compete with man for a share of the vanishing wilderness.

PRECEDING PAGE: Hikers looking toward Zealand Notch in the White Mountains of New Hampshire

slabs, have fallen together to create overhangs and caves, ready-made for wild animals remaining in the region.

Up the steep sides of the ravine, the vegetation becomes less dense. The dry, steep forest floor, well covered with leaves and needles, shows only patches of moss where rocks outcrop. Hemlocks stand alone, virtually the only species of tree on these inclines.

Such is the lasting feeling of Connecticut: a walk through thickset groves of hemlock and beech. Little light breaks into the deepest ravines; one gets the impression of a jungle gorge with steep cliffs and ledges, and of giant logs and boulders tumbled along the sides. In these cool places, protected from wind and sun, leaves have fallen onto rock ledges and soil has formed; from such patches, however meager, grow ferns, herbaceous plants and even young trees. Water slides over ledges into rock-lined pools. And then at night, when your bed is made and the time has come to crawl into your sleeping bag, the sliding and dripping is just outside the shelter as you close your eyes and listen.

The Trail swings north into Massachusetts at Sage's Ravine, crosses Mount Everett, passes beautiful Benedict Pond, and winds through farm and mountain country until it approaches the tops of the Berkshires. The Berkshires do not form an immense range. Areas of wilderness here are not extensive, either, for no point is more than a day's pack trip from some city or village. But that is enough. The size of the wilderness does not necessarily determine how readily a man may lose himself in it.

Hiking over Mount Greylock itself (3,491 feet at the summit) is a pleasure of pleasures, for The Appalachian Trail remains confined and narrow, most often a tunnel through forests of hardwoods, spruce, and balsam fir, reminiscent of the Great Smoky Mountains and characteristic of Canada. Except for rocky ridges, scarcely a patch of bare ground is visible along the Trail. Our footsteps fall on mosses, ferns and grasses, or on soft mats made by an endless fall of leaves. And here again we meet our friend, the oxalis.

For the casual hiker, Mount Greylock has an enticing trail system of its own. Part of an old carriage road remains near the summit, and when strewn with the fresh yellow leaves of autumn birch, it affords one of the most compelling and colorful forest walks we know.

Still, it is not a walk such as our ancestors might have had. They walked through groves of giant beech, alive with squirrels and passenger pigeons. Thousands of chestnut trees reached majestically to the higher hilltops, and enormous specimens of white pine shaded their way.

In early Massachusetts, however, the demands for lumber—hardwood and softwood alike—were enormous. Trees went into the making of railroad ties and split-rail fences; they provided firewood for homes, bark for tanneries, beams to shore up tunnels in mines, and fuel for all-night fires of the charcoal makers. At one time there were 38 tanneries and 185 sawmills in the Berkshires alone.

Down came the giants. Out went the pigeons. In came cattle and sheep. Away went topsoil to the sea.

The Indians vanished, too. Long before white man saw the Berkshires the Indians held them in reverence and felt in consonance with the animals, the waterfalls, and the beauty of the forest. But Indians, like mountains, were "barriers" to be conquered. The Indians lost their rights and their lands to the oncoming settlers, soldiers, explorers and missionaries. Like the mountains, they were tamed. Or they were converted or shot. One way or another, their lands were pre-empted.

But just as the frontier was "won," it moved on. The vast resources of western lands overwhelmed the old economy of the Berkshire country and the natural consequence was a breakdown of the local self-sufficiency of the pioneer. His way of life would change, as the Indian's had.

The men who came after this, victims of whatever circumstances then existed, gave proof of being inspired by the mountains. Oliver Wendell Holmes spent summers in his youth on the family farm near Pittsfield, curled up with a book in the branches of a big pine tree, or visiting such neighbors as Nathaniel Hawthorne and Henry Longfellow. Herman Melville wrote *Moby Dick* in Pittsfield. William Cullen Bryant tramped these hills. And there were Fanny Kemble and Catherine Sedgwick and Edith Wharton. Jonathan Edwards wrote his greatest works in Stockbridge, including *Freedom of the Will.*

Appropriate indeed! This and all kinds of freedoms are what one feels when enjoying the views from the summit of Mount Greylock—valleys stretching north and south; sharply plunging ravines and ridges to the west; range upon range of hills to the east. If there is anything to be called "the real Massachusetts," anything to match Cape Cod in distinctiveness, it is this mountain.

The Berkshires are still sometimes assaulted by the American spirit of "conquest," and here, too, The Appalachian Trail has been in trouble.

In the Berkshires, skiing had its start during the Depression, when ski boots, bindings, poles and other equipment were all but unknown in Pittsfield. Mount Greylock had no lodge and few trails suitable for skiing. But if there were ever a meteoric rise of a sport in the United States, even under the strictures of the Depression, it was this one.

Ski trains brought thousands of city dwellers to the hills. Multitudes of neophytes gained sufficient ski instruction to imbue them with an urge to fly across the snow and down the slopes. CCC crews cut the Thunderbolt, Bellows Pipe and Stony Ledge trails on Greylock, as well as others, and improved certain roads and shelters. But the appetite was not at all satisfied; it was only whetted.

Ski events attracted thousands in any weather and any temperature, and the sport took off like a jumper from a chute. Inevitably came the ski tows. The first one south of Vermont went into service late in 1935, and from then on, the commercial, physical and esthetic values of the sport were established.

Like postmen and hikers, skiers are stopped in their appointed rounds by nothing so simple as rain or snow or sleet. They are, in their own words, infected by a special kind of insanity. Mountains were made for skiing, of course, and the faster you get to the top of a mountain, the more time you have to ski down it. What would be better, therefore, than getting to the top of the highest mountain in one of the most populous eastern states? The idea itself had a ring of challenge.

The wonder is that Greylock did not long ago have a ski tow and wide runs gashed into the forest along its sides. Mount Greylock Reservation was, and is, a state park—but that didn't seem to matter. Demands for ski tows persisted. To counter them, the Mount Greylock Protective Association was organized. The Appalachian Mountain Club also came to the defense, resolutely opposed to further encroachment that would harm the wilderness values of the reservation. These groups, together with the legislature and a majority of the public, have kept developments subdued, but they dare not relax their vigil against continuous, well-endowed schemes to sabotage the wilderness of the mountain.

Some conservationists claim that the mountain is already violated. There is a towering monument to Massachusetts' war dead, but the monument is decaying and crumbling; it has been stained by the elements, and has DANGER—KEEP OUT signs on all four sides. If this lacks dignity as a memorial to the dead, then conservationists can suggest another: a mountaintop as free and undisturbed as the souls of the departed, a peak without ski tows, without monuments, without lodges—nature unsullied. There is nothing as eternal and clean and magnificent as a natural mountain peak to commemorate man's enduring accomplishments. The preservation of a habitat where a rare thrush may sing has more implications of human greatness than the tallest tower on earth.

It was here in Massachusetts that the idea for The Appalachian Trail was first put into action. The long and fascinating history of the Trail is told in excellent detail in publications of the Appalachian Trail Conference and need not be repeated here. The essence of it is that Benton MacKaye, a forester and philosopher from Shirley Center, Massachusetts, wrote and published an article, "The Appalachian Trail—An Experiment in Regional Planning," in the October, 1921, issue of the *Journal* of the American Institute of Architects. A few extended trails were already in existence; the Crawford Path, in New Hampshire, for one, was 100 years old. But the big, long, open-end trail was MacKaye's idea.

For reasons that would in themselves bear sociological research, it seemed to be the right idea at the right time, and caught on with such astonishing rapidity as to surprise even devotees of the Trail. The first mile was cut and marked in 1922 at Palisades Interstate Park, New York. On August 15, 1937, barely fifteen years later, the final sections were finished and the 2,000-mile length of the Trail completed.

Not that there weren't setbacks and periods of languor, but these seemed always to be offset by dedicated leaders with a missionary zeal for seeing the project through. The secret lay in arousing enthusiasm of others, and how well it worked the approximately 100 clubs in the Appalachian Trail Conference bear witness today. There was even a song about the Trail composed and copyrighted six years before the Trail was completed.

The project was exactly what its proponents called it—a mammoth amateur recreational project. It was another example of the work of a few thousands benefiting the lives of millions to come. It may be trite to say, but it is honest: the builders of the Trail were as altruistic as their project. Some of them, like Myron Avery, Chairman of the Appalachian Trail Conference for twenty-one years, are looked upon as heroes; if there is ever a hiker's Hall of Fame, Avery should be among the first to be nominated.

And today—how many people use the Trail? Figures are not available except in a few instances where agencies administering the Trail within parks and forests have made limited counts and issued estimates, and where heavy use is being experienced at Trail huts. The Bureau of Outdoor Recreation, in its excellent publication, *Trails for America*, cites figures to suggest that The Appalachian Trail in Great Smoky Mountains National Park alone attracts more than 100,000 hikers annually, and says that "user visits" along the entire A.T. may total as many as one million in a single year.

And what is more, The Appalachian Trail is an idea that is generating other ideas. Congressional proposals for a national system of foot trails started as early as 1945, but trail pioneers did not wait for legislation; that could catch up later. The Long Trail in Vermont runs 250 miles from Massachusetts to Canada and is over sixty years old (The Appalachian Trail follows the southern third of it). The John Muir Trail in California passes through high country between Yosemite and Sequoia National Parks, a distance of 200 miles. The route of the Pacific Crest Trail extends from Mexico to Canada for 2,313 miles along the Sierras and Cascades. A 350-mile trunk trail, called the Finger Lakes Trail, now being established, will link the Catskills and Allegheny Mountains in New York, and extend across the base of the Finger Lakes to Niagara, where it will connect with the Bruce Trail of Canada.

The National Trails System Act of 1968 established The Appalachian Trail and The Pacific Crest Trail as the first two National Scenic Trails, but also provided for the establishment of recreation and connecting trails. Furthermore, the Secretaries of Interior and Agriculture were authorized to make additional studies of trails that could be added to the nationwide system. Such studies would involve routes, status, acquisition, development plans, maintenance, administration, costs and benefits. The full cooperation of interested state, local, public and private organizations, as well as landowners and land users, was deemed essential. Thus the plans for a nationwide trail system proceed, and none too soon. The question of available land is uncomfortably urgent.

Among new routes under consideration are the Chisholm Trail, of cowboy fame, from San Antonio, Texas, to Abilene, Kansas, 700 miles; the Continental Divide Trail along the Rockies from Mexico to Canada, 3,100 miles; the North Country Trail, from Vermont to North Dakota, 3,200 miles; the Oregon Trail, from Independence, Missouri, to Fort Vancouver, Washington, 2,000 miles; the Natchez Trace, from Nashville, Tennessee, to Natchez, Mississippi, 600 miles; the Potomac Heritage Trail, from the mouth to the source of the Potomac River, 825 miles; and the Santa Fe Trail, from Independence, Missouri, to Santa Fe, New Mexico, 800 miles. One of the longest proposed is the Lewis and Clark Trail, from St. Louis to the Oregon coast, which would include both the outgoing and incoming routes of the famed expedition, a total of 4,600 miles.

A few of the other trails under study are the Pacific Coast Trail, Upper Colorado River Trail, Rio Grande International Trail, Great

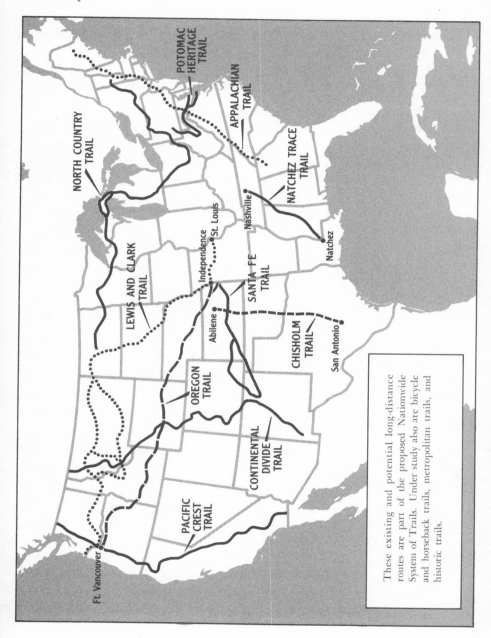

These existing and potential long-distance routes are part of the proposed Nationwide System of Trails. Under study also are bicycle and horseback trails, metropolitan trails, and historic trails.

Lakes International Trail, Mississippi River Trail, Ozarks Trail, Gulf Coast Trail, Atlantic Coast Trail, the Trail of Tears, De Soto Trail, Gold Rush Trail and Mormon Trail.

The demand is not just for hiking trails, either. Bicycling and horse-back riding are sports that need unobstructed, elongated distances. Thus desert irrigation canal banks are being made available for riders and hikers. Wisconsin has opened a 297-mile bikeway across the entire state, the first of its kind in the United States. Abandoned railroad rights of way are being developed for recreation, as in the case of the Prairie Path for a distance of forty miles west of Chicago. Open spaces beneath utility lines are sites of obvious value, as are river channels when not in use for flood control.

Most of these latter are multiple-purpose trails not necessarily concerned with the environment. They are for physical exercise, recreation, and sports, and their location is of lesser consequence than in the case of wilderness trails.

Nor is the United States the sole possessor of long trails. Walking, as we know, has long been a favorite pastime in Great Britain. Hobbes walked for health and pleasure. So did John Stuart Mill, Samuel Johnson and Boswell, Keats, Matthew Arnold, George Meredith, Robert Louis Stevenson, John Ruskin, and William H. Hudson. Coleridge talks of walking forty miles a day, and during one walk composed the first stanzas of "The Ancient Mariner." Carlyle once did fifty-four miles in a single day. Ben Jonson, at the height of his fame, made a celebrated walking trip to Scotland, and was royally entertained wherever be went. Dickens loved night walks and often came home tired at sunrise. Scott, lame as he was, walked twenty or thirty miles a day, and even climbed, pulling himself up with his arms when his legs failed. Shakespeare apparently preferred the footpath with stiles to the road or moor, but Shelley climbed over nearly everything.

Probably Wordsworth holds the record for accumulated mileage. De Quincey says of him: "I calculate, upon good data, that with these identical legs Wordsworth must have traversed a distance of 175,000 or 180,000 English miles, a mode of exertion which to him stood in the stead of alcohol and all stimulants whatsoever to the animal spirits; to which indeed he was indebted for a life of unclouded happiness, and we for much of what is most excellent in his writings."

Had there been a long trail in England in the days of these stalwarts, some of them probably would have hiked it. Now there is such a trail, and England can rejoice.

On April 24, 1965, more than 3,000 people gathered on the moors near Malham Tarn, in Yorkshire Dales National Park, to celebrate completion of public right of way along the 250-mile length of Britain's first long-distance footpath—the Pennine Way. The Minister of Land and Natural Resources was there, and so was Tom Stephenson, Secretary of the Ramblers' Association, who first promoted the idea thirty years before.

It was a great day for Tom Stephenson and for England. The Pennine Way runs from the Peak District National Park of Derbyshire, 150 miles northwest of London, to the Cheviot Hills, on the Scottish border. Following existing footpaths, shepherds' and miners' trails, bridleways, drove roads, and old Roman roads, it passes through some of the wildest and roughest country in Britain.

The trail makes its way through expanses of heather or moor grass, over the boggy plateau of Kinder Scout and the wilderness of Bleaklow. Traversing the moors of the Brontë country, it goes into the lowlands of Craven and across the green fields and gray limestone walls of Malham in the Yorkshire Dales National Park. It follows the line of a Roman Road, the Maiden Way, up to Hadrian's Wall, and ultimately along Agricola's road from York to Scotland.

The Pennine Way is not all. Rights of way are being acquired for ten approved long-distance paths totaling more than 1,250 miles.

In Canada, there is the Bruce Trail, from Niagara Falls to Tobermory on Georgian Bay. Still in the process of clearing, it will be about four hundred miles long when completed. The route has already been walked, however, by one well-known pedestrian, John Muir, a century ago.

South Africa has long trails, and Germany has its famous Black Forest paths. In Norway, the hiker can travel from fiord to fiord, stay at a different hut each night, and return to his destination via different fiords or by ferries, bus or train; the trails are in a network that permits the advantage of round trips.

Sweden has many hiking routes, including the *Kungsleden*, or Royal Route, in northern Lappland, 430 kilometers (270 miles) long. The Swedish Touring Club provides facilities for travelers in Swedish mountain areas of Lappland, Jämtland, Härjedalen and Dalarna. These facilities include the *kåta*, a conical Lapp-style hut with turf-covered sides; the *fjällstuga*, consisting usually of two rooms; and the *fjällstation*, a more elaborate hostel. Excellent maps and booklets—some in English —are available from the Club: Svenska Turistföreningens Resebyrå, Stureplan 2, Fack, Stockholm 7, Sweden.

The idea is growing.

"I have two doctors," said Trevelyan, "my left leg and my right." It is good to know that people with the same sensibilities as Trevelyan can hike and climb in more countries than one, that The Appalachian Trail hiker belongs to an international brotherhood of *frères du piste*.

It is also good to know that the hiker's simple wish for a clear path, reasonably free of ski lifts, free of parallel highways, free of reservoirs, is being more and more honored as time goes on. Perhaps, after all, time is on his side. The national system of trails will reach into the lives and uplift the health and spirits of millions to come. Those who pioneered The Appalachian Trail, who maintain it and who hike it, ought to be feeling pretty proud these days.

Two roads diverged in a wood, and I—
I took the one less traveled by,
And that has made all the difference.

Robert Frost

A Planetary Feeling

"The surface of Vermont," wrote Zadock Thompson in his 1842 history of the State, "is generally uneven."

Uneven is the word for the Green Mountains. We climbed into them on an autumn morning, headed for what has been called one of the most beautiful lakes in Vermont.

At first we followed an abandoned road, where dense vegetation came down to the edge of the path. Then the trail curved around the slope of a hill in more open forest, and dropped into a ravine, where we crossed a stream.

We followed this stream uphill, past rapids and waterfalls, step by step with the sounds of tumbling water. The whole woods scene seemed alive that morning, and a flood of sounds reached our ears: the drift of wind in the tops of the trees, the rustle of leaves, the warnings of squirrels. As always, the notes and calls of birds reminded us of the adage: "A bird in the hand is worth two in the bush—but a bird in the bush may sing." Had anyone at that moment asked for our favorite impression of traveling on The Appalachian Trail, we would have answered: sounds.

We remembered the acorns dropping with riflelike reports on the

119

trail back at Bear Mountain State Park in New York, the chickadees in Deans Ravine, the chatter of juncos, the shout of flickers, the warning of hawks, and the call of loons. In a single day on the Trail we had gotten to know more songs of warblers than in a month at home. In the mountain forest were melodies of veery and thrush, and on a quiet path —as in the Smokies—the sound of the drumming grouse.

These things are missed by persons riding along a highway. Like the mythical Ixion, they are tied to the wheel. They cannot hear the drumming of grouse or the music of this little stream beside the trail. Nor can they see the remote and hidden mountain ponds reached only by trail.

"The waters of the lakes, ponds, and streams," continued Zadock Thompson, "are universally soft, miscible with soap, and in general free from foreign substances."

People still talk of these lakes and ponds as if they were jewels. There are not many ponds along the A.T. south of New England, but from here to Maine we came to know them well.

A few miles south of Rutland, in Green Mountain National Forest, lay one of the loveliest of all. Even The Appalachian Trail Guide to Vermont refers to Little Rock Pond as one of the prettiest lakes in the state, which is saying a great deal. Anxious to see it, we walked as rapidly as we could—but on The Appalachian Trail that was never very fast.

Our senses were assaulted by the sights, the sounds, the smells, the feeling, even the tastes of the wild. Everywhere there was color and motion and form, and it seemed as though our eyes could not move fast enough to take in everything, or would wear out before the day came to an end.

Most often our eyes fell on the trail itself, patched with sunlight and tinted with the first fallen leaves of autumn. Maple leaves, explosive in their red intensity, turned the trail into a crimson path, or other leaves converted it to glowing gold. Sometimes there were leaves fallen upside down, exposing an almost iridescent purple laced with reddish veins. Except for the coolness of the forest, we might have been walking on fire.

Vermont and New Hampshire in autumn offer some of the finest hiking on The Appalachian Trail. By September the fringes of sugar maples have begun to yellow, and some trees here and there, like early renegades from summer's green, have advanced to a brilliant red.

"It seems to me," says Maurice Brooks, "that I have never seen the maples and birches as blazing elsewhere as they appear in and around New England's and New York's famous notches. Wilmington Notch in New York, Smugglers in Vermont, and any of the eight or so best known in New Hampshire are often at their peak of color during the first ten days of October."

In places the Trail followed long-abandoned logging roads. As almost everywhere else, beds of oxalis grew beside the Trail; asters and goldenrod bloomed, and now we came to patches of dwarf dogwood. The viburnums, bearing clusters of scarlet berries, wore dark leaves with splotches of royal maroon intersected by greenish veins.

There were few or no mosquitoes at this season—in fact, hardly any insects at all. The air was clear and quiet. Distances were almost unobstructed by haze, and the nights already had begun to turn cold.

Clear days occur in summer, too, and on one such day in Vermont the idea for The Appalachian Trail was born.

"In the summer of 1900," wrote Benton MacKaye in a letter to the Appalachian Trail Conference in 1964, "with my old woods partner Horace Hildreth of Harvard, Mass., I covered the high points of the Green Mountains from Haystack to Mansfield. This was ten years before the start of the Long Trail. We walked up through the trailless woods to the top of Stratton Mountain and climbed trees in order to see the view.

"It was a clear day with a brisk breeze blowing. North and south sharp peaks etched the horizon. I felt as if atop the world, with a sort of 'planetary feeling.' I seemed to perceive peaks far southward, hidden by old Earth's curvature. Would a footpath someday reach them from where I was then perched? Little did I dream. . . ."

But he did dream, and he had put his dreams to work. Uphill beside the little stream, we hiked and thought about his "planetary feeling," and the Trail that had come from it. Twenty years after his walk to

Stratton Mountain, MacKaye developed and published his plea for an open-end path. And less than twenty years after that The Appalachian Trail was open to travelers.

We stopped and spread our pemmican, meat bars and chocolate on a rock beside the trail and enjoyed a lunch as welcome and delicious as any in the finest salon.

The more the hiker gets to know the wilderness, the more refined do his senses of taste and smell become. The Appalachian Trail, above all, passes through lands where freshness is the chief sensation. In the air, the trees, even in decaying leaves, there is the constant, detectable freshness of life and growth. A pervading odor of dankness symbolizes enrichment and renewal, and the refreshment of falling rain is never far away. Had anyone asked at lunch about our favorite impression of walking along the trail, we would have said: the wonderful freshness of the Appalachian forests.

Spruce and fir add a delightful tang to this environment. The oak community has special odors, as do the swamps, the rivers, and the open balds. In spring, the Appalachians are touched with a special fragrance of flowers. The mists of summer have their distinctive scents, and the icy autumn winds have theirs.

The hiker without a sense of smell would not have nearly as rich a trip as he does—rich with the savory smoke of campfires, the outdoor aroma of trout or bacon frying for breakfast, the pungency of coffee in front of the lean-to.

How successfully our automobiles and homes insulate us from this! The hiker is in a world of his own.

And what of taste? When we had finished our pemmican and moved on up the trail toward Little Rock Pond, we talked of strawberries in Tennessee, raspberries in Maine, blackberries in the lowlands of Virginia, and blueberries nearly everywhere along the Trail.

A hiker who knows which plants are edible could literally live off the land—and be a gourmet at that. For salads he has a choice of leaves and shoots, tubers, petals, roots, pods and sprouts. For vegetables he may gather mustard greens, wild lettuce and onion, water cress, day lily, cattail and cow parsnip. Certain grasses are delicious, and so is the bark of selected trees. Wild rice and sunflower seeds are renewable natural resources, there to be harvested by man or beast. For spices, one has a choice of ginger, caraway, peppergrass, horseradish, mint, and bayberry. Snacks can be made from hickories, acorns, beechnuts, hazelnuts, and pine seeds. Dessert may be chosen from maple sugar or any of dozens of wild fruits, including plums, persimmons, cherries, elderberries, serviceberries, grapes, May apple, wild raisin and pawpaw. And to top off a wilderness meal, there are sassafras tea, birch beer, or various substitutes for coffee and chocolate.

When these are added to the basic and special foods carried on his back, the hiker needs no one to be concerned about him. What restaurant has foods any fresher than those plucked here at the edge of the trail?

And what of the glorious, simple taste of water? When you bend down to the pool that is lined with grass and moss and oxalis and drink the cold, refreshing water of a spring—or unhitch your cup from your belt and dip it into an icy natural fountain or waterfall—you know that princes never had more satisfying elixir.

But the experienced hiker also knows that, for all the rain and moisture, for all the richness of the forest he does not take for granted that there is water everywhere. Sometimes springs are scarce, and a few moments of wisdom in planning hikes around the existence of sources of water prevents cruel hours of thirst while hiking.

For a long time we ascended a rise through the woods and finally came to a mountain pass. Not far beyond, as the Trail dropped slightly, we saw an expanse of white. By now the sky had become overcast with haze; the forest had a dimmer aspect and it was surprising to come upon whiteness instead of darkness through the trees. Puzzled, we walked a little faster until we realized that we were looking at the surface of a lake reflecting the white of the sky. We had arrived at Little Rock Pond.

It lay cupped in a basin below Green Mountain, which rose rock ribbed and covered with spruce to an elevation of 2,509 feet. The lower slopes, as well as the pond, were girt with hardwoods that seemed to be marching in a colorful procession of purple, yellow, red and brown to the water's edge, and bending over the pond as if to get a drink. Some, in fact, had fallen in.

The pond was not very large; a person could walk around it in twenty minutes. But around Little Rock Pond there are no reasons for hurrying.

The quiet and solitude were perfect complements to the scene. We lingered to capture the view, to soak up the silence, to feel the fresh wind blowing across the water. Overhead, dark clouds had begun to gather and their boiling shapes of gray and black added a special excitement to the environment of the pond. The sounds of rustling foliage now began to fill the forest, and red and yellow leaves flew out like waterfowl to land on the surface of the lake.

On the northwest side of the pond was a tiny island, sufficient to support some trees, a shelter and two tables. If we were to judge a contest to see which shelter on The Appalachian Trail lay in the most dreamlike setting, this one would reach the finals. We had to see it; so walking on grassy banks or through underbrush and climbing over cliffs of light-colored schist, we went around the edge of the pond, through woods on the western side across a small plank bridge and finally onto the island.

When we reached the shelter we saw that it was occupied, though the tenants themselves happened to be absent. Where they were we had no way of knowing. We looked around. Inside the shelter lay two plastic bags about six feet long, each stuffed with moss and ferns. Extra shoes, canvas, towels and other paraphernalia had been placed to one side.

The shelter faced out on the pond and on the sides and back was hemmed in by trees and shrubs. There was room, however, for two camp tables, one in front of the shelter and one at the side. These were bare except for a single object on each: a package of pipe tobacco on one and a can of Metrecal on the other.

By now the clouds had gathered their fury into a storm, and high winds were making waves from the placid waters of the pond. To the south, a mass of gray-black clouds approached, and we knew to our great delight that we were going to be caught in a storm.

Scarcely had we completed our circuit of Little Rock Pond and moved into the woods along the A.T. when the cloudburst broke. Immediately the forest was filled with a lashing rain that whipped the branches furiously. Every leaf had a different motion. Every tall tree seemed to bend as far as it could in different directions, as if trying to flee. Leaves blew along the trail in whirling succession.

We took a last look at Little Rock Pond, then turned and went down the Trail. Rain blew into our faces with the coolness and refreshment that one gets nowhere else than in a clean and glorious mountain storm.

The sense of touch, of feeling, may be for some hikers the quintessence of a trip down the Trail. This "touch" might be the pressure of pack straps on the shoulders, or fatigue in the muscles, or the hot, moist fever at the temples after a long stretch of uphill climbing, or the solid pounding of the heart. Clean work! Clean sweat!

Few but the hiker will understand this reverence for exertion. The more he gets, the more he seems to want. Yet somehow when he emerges sunburnt and squint eyed, dusty, muddy, and tired, perhaps even exhausted to the core, he feels an unexplainable sense of satisfaction.

Perhaps the zenith of his tactual experiences is achieved when he finds an idyllic pool along a stream, when he strips his warm and pounding body, and slips into the water, its coolness sliding over his skin and bringing with it a delirious refreshment for which there is no substitute.

Other sensations occur within him every hour, every minute: chills along his spine when a grouse or quail flies suddenly up in front or when a moose goes crashing through the undergrowth in the north woods; horrifying suspense when a boulder on which he is stepping gives way without warning beneath his feet; a pleasant sense of accomplishment when the end of the trail nears. Outside, he feels the soft sweep of a summer mist; the cutting cold of an early winter wind; the roughness of the trail. He may stand at the edge of a bog, with feet sinking into the sphagnum moss. On a promontory he sees a road below and regrets the necessity that keeps his fellow creatures in their automobiles, which appear so small from this vantage point. In such moments the hiker is likely to recall the saying that the automobile is a toy for adults. He may indeed see little poetry in a moving car.

In any case, Little Rock Pond and the Trail that led to it made indelible impressions upon our minds and senses. It was another personal discovery. The whole A.T. is one long series of discoveries waiting for hikers with eyes to see and ears to hear; it is in fact a feast for all the senses, and it doesn't take long for the hiker to develop a special perceptivity. One pond such as Little Rock Pond, one stream, one breath of wind in the highlands, and he has the "Seeing Eye" that Margaret Farrand wrote about:

> A curve in the road and a hillside,
> Clear cut against the sky,
> A tall tree tossed by the autumn wind
> And a white cloud riding high.
> Ten men went along that road
> And all but one passed by.
> He saw the hill and the tree and the cloud
> With an artist's mind and eye,
> And he put them down on canvas
> For the other nine men to buy.

Robert Frost would have called such a man a sensibilitist. Frost knew the mountains well. He lived near Franconia, New Hampshire, with his family for five years following his return from England in 1915. He wanted to live where he could see the mountains—and here he could, every day—the Presidentials, the Twins, Garfield, Scarface, Big Bickford, the ledges of Eagle Cliff. There was Franconia Notch, with Lafayette and Cannon forming its ramparts.

Here he produced his third volume of poems, *Mountain Interval*.

Mountains were always a part of Robert Frost's horizons, and none more than those of Franconia. And he wanted them kept as they were. "The more the sensibilitist I am," he wrote, "the more I seem to want my mountains wild. . . . I'd hate to be a runaway from nature."

Wherever one hikes, he finds the touches of those who have gone before, and knows that this is a shared trail. Others have gone before him and he sees the evidence of their passing. Once we came to a Vermont shelter that was constructed of stone, with a broken concrete floor, a few ripped fragments of screens, torn plastic window coverings and bunks with patched wire mesh. To the highway traveler accustomed to tiled motels and glassed-in restaurants, this might have looked very dreary indeed. On the contrary, there were two fireplaces which, when stoked and lighted, must have warmed the cold gray walls for many a hiker. But the touch that had taken away all bleakness was on a fireplace mantle. Someone in the past had placed two beer cans there, one on each side, into which had been stuffed bouquets of wild flowers and a tasteful arrangement of branches containing berries.

Another Vermont shelter, tended with loving care by a husband-and-wife maintenance crew, contained a full array of helpful equipment: table, ashtray (a can lid), candle in a bottle, two tin cups, stove, saw, axe, rake, bucket, broom, shovel, dustpan, rope, clothes hangers, salt, sugar, kindling, even a discarded sleeping bag and an excellent pair of hiking breeches. On the table lay a pencil and a register book, with these comments:

"September 16. We came in with sore feet and aching bodies. The Lodge was certainly a welcome sight. Many thanks to our predecessors for their 'touches of home.' Started out last Saturday from Williamstown, Massachusetts and expect to reach Sherbourne Pass by next Saturday. We had some showers during the afternoon and the temperature has been on the cool side. We just learned today that the Space Twins landed safely last Sunday."

"September 5. Our first wedding anniversary and also the first

Appalachian lodge we have ever seen; both are wonderful. Out for this beautiful walk, fully appreciating the glorious beauties of nature and God."

"September 9. The Taj Mahal has nothing on this little palace!! I love it! Time to hit the trail again. We'll be back."

"September 11. Up here for weekend and having a great time. No porkies yet but we're hoping. Had trouble finding dead wood try the oithere side of the streem. Latreen's all right but someone should paint the seets another color [they were bright blue and chewed by porcupines].

"After having fallen down the side of Camel's Hump, I consider myself a Long Trail veteran. Wether I'm entitled to a pension or not I don't know; maybe three porcupine hides a year."

[And then in a different handwriting:] "Actually he didn't fall he jumped so we could take him in town for a hot meal and chance to sit on a paded chair in the doctors office."

And in a cryptic vein, this entry, in its entirety: "September 12, 1965 . . . a while later . . . 11:10 A.M. . . . a somewhat dreary but excellent-for-hiking Sunday . . . autumn leaves lining wet and mossy trail . . . dripping diamonds from newly drenched leaves . . . ethnic candle burning . . . dripping must go on . . . can't help but wonder where we're bound. . . ."

North of Little Rock Pond, The Appalachian Trail swings east over Killington Peak and leaves the Long Trail, which it has been following up through the center of Vermont, and which is itself "three or four weeks long." There has been little time to take notice of what this land has meant to others before us, but we thus risk missing some high adventures. This land meant a great deal to the brothers Allen—Ethan and Ira—in Revolutionary days. Best known was Ethan, the blustering, swaggering hero of Fort Ticonderoga, and leader of the freewheeling Green Mountain Boys, who defended independent Vermont against the claims of Colonial New York.

Ethan led an attack on Montreal, but was captured and kept for almost three years in England. His brother Ira helped frame the

Hut boys backpacking the supplies that make it possible for hikers to tour the Presidential Range relatively unencumbered, supported by the system of huts maintained by the Appalachian Mountain Club

Hikers getting advice on trail conditions from a Forest Ranger at the Appalachian Mountain Club's Pinkham Notch Camp in New Hampshire

PRECEDING PAGE: A lone hiker at the edge of the Great Gulf Wild Area, in the White Mountain National Forest

Hikers above Little Rock Pond in Vermont. There is a secluded trail shelter on the small island.

Vermont constitution (Vermont was for 14 years an independent republic) and served as her first treasurer.

The Allens engaged in a tricky game of politics by trying to play the United States against Canada, and ultimately they were suspected of trying to deliver Vermont back to the British. They fell from authority, Ethan dying at Burlington in 1789, still a popular hero; and Ira, in poverty, years later in Philadelphia. Ironically, three Vermont towns are named for Ira, but none for Ethan.

We enter New Hampshire. Here The Appalachian Trail follows trails in existence long before it came into being. First are trails of the Dartmouth Outing Club. Beyond Mount Moosilauke, trails of the Appalachian Mountain Club are followed through the White Mountains. Here we cross a string of landmarks: Mount Moosilauke, Franconia Notch and its famed Old Man, and Crawford Notch. The Appalachian Trail then rises into the highest of New Hampshire's Presidential Range (Mounts Monroe, Washington, Jefferson, Adams and Madison) and some of the most spectacular hiking on the entire Trail.

The White Mountains come upon you as a slowly dawning surprise. First there is the foreground, the deeply and richly forested foothills that give no hint of the towering masses beyond. Then there are vague and mysterious shapes far ahead, ill-defined in the haze. After a while you notice an outline ahead, through the trees, of a ridge going up and up and up, its summit hidden by distance and topographic configuration.

It is at this moment that you begin to discover the one great fact of the White Mountains: their immensity.

You rise as the trail rises, past rocks blanketed with moss, through groves of birch and maple and spruce, into the higher, thinner, purer air. The rocks become more jagged and exposed, for in the upper regions they lie tumbled and broken by frost; they are also twisted by time into extraordinary contortions. And then, above 4,500 feet, the forest thins out and becomes more stunted until the limit of trees has passed. With this, you have achieved what was impossible in the Great Smokies: you have risen above tree line.

In nearly all directions the barren summits, gray and dignified, some-times brooding or dark or wrapped and hidden in clouds, surround you. The masses are enormous. Great ravines and "gulfs" fall away from the ridges with a deep and sometimes precipitous sweep of talus and forest. Your eyes follow them to openings in the ridges and through these to the New Hampshire farmlands far in the distance.

To hike here is to walk on top of the world. You become elated, more elated than usual, your spirit released from some indefinite con-finement just as your body has been released from the forest. Nature here, as at the Grand Canyon of Arizona, is too big to understand, and you feel free from the need to try.

You feel utterly free. You have more confidence—in nature, in the world, in your own capacity to succeed. Your tired feet and aching muscles, as if by some strange magic, renew their energy, and it seems as if you could go on hiking for as long as the trail lasts.

Soon, however, like the dawning of a wondrous surprise, you realize that the magic is not strange at all. It is the old magic of climbing in the mountains, something forgotten in the valley, and the magic of a trail that leads from one rediscovery to another.

Here in the White Mountains, The Appalachian Trail is once again partly on protected public land—White Mountain National Forest—and partly on private land. There are more than a thousand miles of foot trails within the National Forest itself, giving excellent access into these folded and upended lands of bear and deer, moose, rabbit, grouse and other animals. To give special protection to a segment of the wild moun-tains, the Forest Service established the Great Gulf Wilderness Area in 1959. The Gulf, a spectacular glacier-carved valley on the eastern slopes of the Presidential Range, contains streams, cascades, lakes, and deep corners difficult of access. One feels remoteness here, though elsewhere—and not so far away—the mountains are being used with vigor and are becoming increasingly valuable for a variety of forms of outdoor recre-ation.

The Dartmouth Outing Club and the Appalachian Mountain Club both maintain trails and shelters in this region. The latter club was founded in 1876 and hence is the oldest mountain club in the United States. Its eight huts along The Appalachian Trail, in the Franconia, Presidential and Carter Ranges, are ideal for hikers preferring to travel light or to enjoy a few more of the comforts of home than the open, windy slopes provide.

A.M.C. huts range in capacity from forty to more than a hundred persons, and have been so popular and so intensively used (24,000 persons overnight in 1965) that new and better huts are being built. One of the newest is Mizpah Spring hut on Mt. Clinton, erected at an elevation of 3,800 feet and located 2½ miles from the nearest road. It has been designed to withstand heavy mountain snows and winds of up to 200 miles per hour. The building, with a capacity of seventy-two persons, offers food and lodging to anyone, not just members of the Appalachian Mountain Club; indeed, 85 per cent of the use of A.M.C. huts in these mountains is by the general public, which seems to be an exceptionally fine example of public service. Mizpah, like all the huts, is staffed by college men and others who sometimes hoist more than 100 pounds on their backs in order to bring in supplies.

Mount Washington itself has long been a curiosity. The earliest climbers—and this mountain is regarded as the birthplace of American mountain climbing—reverently regarded it as being more than 10,000 feet high; it actually is 6,288. The Indians believed that it was the home of the Great Spirit, and that no one could climb to the top and survive.

They were nearly right, for with winds of hurricane force (75 miles per hour and above) occurring on an average of every other day, and the greatest velocities at the summit exceeding 200 miles per hour (a speed of 231 miles per hour was recorded here in 1934), the ascent of the mountain can be perilous in the extreme.

A hiker may start out with the air still, the leaves scarcely rustling. By the time he has broken out onto the treeless ridges, the wind is blowing fiercely and the temperature has sharply dropped. If he is wearing or carrying no more than a light jacket, the time has come to turn back. In no time at all, the weather can get worse. Winds once blew down a log railway trestle weighing 1,100 pounds per running foot, and the temperature has at times approached 60 degrees below zero. Only a fraction of such extremes is enough to do in a hardy hiker.

The trouble is that the tempests are not all local in origin, and thus may not be as transitory as a summer squall. Disturbances from the Great Lakes and the Gulf of Mexico occasionally meet here and the resulting storms may be reinforced by gales from Atlantic shores not far away.

At the base of the mountain are signs that warn all hikers to turn back if they are unprepared or if there is the slightest indication of dangerous weather. Storms rise with phenomenal rapidity now and then, and there have been numerous deaths caused by exhaustion and exposure; the moral is to carry or wear adequate clothing, any time of the year, when heading into this range or above tree line anywhere in New England.

There have been many hikers who failed to return alive, for the elements rage on Mount Washington as on few other places. "To sample the world's worst weather," said a former director of the Harvard-Blue Hill Observatory, "spend a winter on Mount Washington. At least, the mountain can dish up the worst combination of cold, wind, and blowing snow to be found at any permanently inhabited place on earth." Bradford Washburn, the polar explorer, agrees; except for some isolated peaks in the Arctic and Antarctic, he says, this mountain has the most severe weather in the world.

Still, in its milder manner the mountain has attracted countless numbers of famous persons, including Emerson, Hawthorne, Thoreau, Whittier, Louisa May Alcott, Daniel Webster, James Russell Lowell and Charles Sumner. A land so appealing in shape and form, and so subtle in colors, should be a natural challenge for artists, and they have come. Winslow Homer painted here. So did Thomas Cole, Thomas Doughty, and John Frederick Kensett of the Hudson River School.

And then there was P. T. Barnum. He called the view from the top "the second greatest show on earth."

Or of the earth, perhaps. As in the Great Smoky Mountains and along the Blue Ridge, the hiker beholds a stage on which has been enacted an overpowering drama of mountains in the making, a place where shapes and forms and heights have been superbly put together. The foundations of these mountains are the result of Appalachian orogeny and erosion for eons, but here in the White Mountains there are distinctive differences.

Like the Great Smokies, the White Mountains were born in an era of time when layers of sediments were accumulating in the depths of an unknown sea. In a slow upheaval, these layers were folded on a gigantic scale and lifted into the prehistoric sky. Original sedimentary structures such as bedding planes were broken, crushed and thoroughly confused in the folding, jointing and fracturing that took place. Minerals formed and reformed, and to complicate the structure further, great volumes of granite were injected into the mountains.

The result was a tightly folded mass of recrystallized schists and quartzites, some of the most compact and weather-resistant rocks in New England.

This has been the secret of the mountains—their resistance. Despite the vast amount and intensity of weathering to which they have been subjected, they have kept their massive prominence.

And it is this weathering that gives the Presidentials their distinction over southerly ranges along The Appalachian Trail.

After long attack by streams and other forms of running water (that great reducer of continents) the Ice Age came, and the White Mountains were covered by glacial ice. First there were local mountain glaciers forming below the summits themselves, growing larger, plucking away debris, widening the valleys in which they formed. Thus were scoured out basins or bowls, called cirques, of which the great Gulf, Tuckerman Ravine, and Huntington Ravine are special examples.

Then came a sea of ice thousands of feet thick, moving south from Canada and covering the face of New England. Thus were the Presidentials engulfed, and in the following centuries they were cut and scratched and striated, etched, rounded, smoothed and otherwise carved by the action of the ice. Boulders were borne from points far away and eventually dumped on higher peaks when the ice sheets melted.

As the climate changed and warmed, the ice sheets stopped and began to waste away, leaving behind deposits of boulders, pebbles, sand and other sediments contained in them. River channels were formed and then abandoned with the further vanishment of the ice. And at last the ice was gone.

Evidence of all this upheaval, erosion and deposition still exists and can be seen along the roads and trails of the White Mountains, though some of the surface striations on higher summits have been blotted out by the action of frost. Water freezing in cracks and crevices on the treeless peaks has caused great blocks of schist and granite to be split off, and the impression of the hiker is that of a tumbled confusion of angular boulders over which hiking would be a challenge indeed without the benefit of trails.

Now, once again, the mountains are subject to erosion by running water and by winter freezing and thawing. The giant cirques are being filled—ever so slowly—with the debris of centuries. The mountains, so resistant to change and yet so temporary in the final analysis, are once more undergoing the kinds of changes that were wrought upon them for millions of years before the mountain and continental glaciers began to move.

And now man. There were many footsteps in these ranges before there were trails or huts. Scarcely a dozen years after the voyage of the *Mayflower* these mountains were discovered and scaled; the North American passion for conquering nature and mountains began early.

The first description of Mount Washington country was written by a traveler named Walter Neal after a visit in 1631 or 1632: "It is a rising ground from the sea-shore to these hills, and they are inaccessible but by gullies which the dissolved snow hath made. In these gullies grow savin [juniper] bushes, which, being taken hold of, are a great help to the climbing discoverer. Upon the top of the highest of these mountains is a large level, or plain, of a day's journey over, whereon nothing grows but moss.

"The country beyond the hills is clambering terrible, being full of rocky hills, as thick as molehills in a meadow, and clothed with infinite thick woods."

Since that day, thousands upon thousands more have gone to the top, some barefoot, some running all the way, some counting the steps (16,925). Others have gone up on a bicycle, or a dogsled. A carriage road was opened in 1861. In 1869 a cog railway was completed to the summit and in that year Ulysses S. Grant made a train trip to the top, first President to do so during his term of office.

Atop Mount Washington, the hiker leaves wilderness behind, for he must share the summit with a hotel, restaurant, rail and highway terminus, weather station, and radio and television transmitters. But going on northward, he soon finds wilderness once more on the other peaks; then across the Androscoggin River, and he climbs into the rugged Mahoosuc Range and the wilderness of Maine.

There is something else new here, too, besides the glacial landscape. "You have the feeling of landmarks in this country," a friend once told us. "From the White Mountains north you hike day after day, and the silhouettes of peaks, like Goose Eye, in Maine, serve as reference points as you progress along the trail. Each day the image of Goose Eye, against the Maine and New Hampshire wilderness, comes into sharper focus; each hour we see it coming closer and growing clearer and a sort of breathless expectancy builds up within us. Likewise, as we go on hiking, the peaks recede as we cast glimpses backward, and in the end they are lost again in the haze and the distance."

Despite their popularity and floods of people, the hiker still finds in New Hampshire's White Mountains his kind of dramatic wilderness. These are mountains for lovers of distance and freedom, and frequently the friendships founded here have lasting benefit.

Justice William O. Douglas thinks of the experience as a fulfillment that makes sweat and toil a joy. "The weary hiker who stays the night," he says, referring to A.M.C. huts, "dines heartily, makes small botanical, geological, or ornithological discoveries in the surrounding country, sees the sun set over distant ridges, and shares in the conviviality of an evening with the hutmen, feels somehow compelled to revisit the huts over and over again. . . .

"The White Mountains, which offer unique hiking trails in a unique wilderness, are the solace and comfort of three million people today. The number who will turn to them, seeking refuge from civilization, will increase in the years immediately ahead. Today the White Mountains are within a day's drive by car for over forty million people. By the end of this century that number will double, and the trails, ponds, shelters, campgrounds, and huts will be increasingly used. With our mounting population, every ridge, every crag, every wooded ravine will have increased value."

And so they will. The hiker says a hearty "Amen."

9

The evergreen woods had a decidedly sweet and bracing fragrance; the air was a sort of diet-drink, and we walked on buoyantly in Indian file, stretching our legs.

Thoreau

A Damp and Intricate Wilderness

At its northern end, The Appalachian Trail passes through deep wilderness country, a mountain fastness comparable in grandeur to the southern highlands, and equally remote and wild. One mile, one curve, one ridge out of earshot of a highway, and you are contemporary and companion of Henry David Thoreau. The twentieth century all but disappears; you drop back into days gone by and your map of Maine is to all intents a scrap of buckskin with an empty circle in the center labeled "Indian Country" or "Unexplored." That, after all, is the idea. That is why the Trail goes through this land where it does.

It was Thoreau's idea, too, and when he arrived in 1847, this northern wilderness was already being reaped of its virgin woods. Maine was originally developed for fishing, furs and shipbuilding, the last of which did more to alter the original scene than all other endeavors (save possibly agriculture). Clear away the land, cut, saw, float—to Thoreau the loggers were so many busy demons bent on driving the forest out of the country, from every solitary beaver swamp and mountainside, as soon as possible. The harvest continued diligently, so that when John Burroughs came upon the scene in the early 1900's, he said that Maine was no longer a "Pine Tree State," and therefore titled his essay "A Taste of Maine Birch."

But for all that, even lacking those glorious groves of great white pine, Maine is yet as Thoreau called it: a damp and intricate wilderness, where nature is ever in her spring. It is still as damp and still as intricate —if it is no longer the wilderness it was.

In Maine, The Appalachian Trail extends for 279 miles through reasonably wild forest, and in places above the forest on barren mountain peaks. It is sometimes a cold and forbidding land. Half of Maine is farther north than Montreal, and the 45th parallel bisects the state, placing it halfway to the North Pole.

It has been much colder than now, for the landscape, as in the White Mountains, has been scoured and ground and polished by glaciation. A vast deciduous forest covering much of eastern North America was severely reduced during the Ice Age. What soil there was has been taken up as if by a giant scoop, the rich humus of yesterage plucked and carted away by glaciers that pulled off fragments of granite, scraped them, scratched them, and tumbled them into worn-out boulders struck with striations. Except for the southern highlands, where the forest continued to flourish, whole mountains were denuded and torn away, bit by bit. Boulders collecting in eddies of ice or left in static melting positions created dams that blocked entire valleys, or became hills, or were piled into ridges. A few original mountains remained, though much reduced. Glaciers had changed the shape and features, and deranged the river patterns, of the land that was to be Maine.

As the glaciers withdrew, the land nurtured a rich coniferous forest, reseeded from the southern highlands, where the forest had grown even richer through the years. Spruce and fir predominated, as still they do, though now there are probably far more numerous patches of maple and birch and beech, or "openings," as they are called.

Walking through these friendly woods brought back to us the feeling of the rain forest. It was a feeling almost as intense as we had known in the Hoh River Valley of western Washington, though nothing here was as intensely green; dark green predominated. The annual precipitation there is usually well above a hundred inches, here not much above forty. And here, the bite of winter is real and fierce. Even so, there is often a fire danger in this heavily wooded wilderness, as there is along the rest of the Trail, which calls for constant vigil on the part of hikers. Maine sometimes has as many as a thousand forest fires a year.

Most of the time, however, the dampness and the intricateness of the wild pervade nearly every step of the Trail. As we hiked, a thousand sights and sounds came to us. They came not in order, but scattered in a complex of experiences so that we rarely knew what to expect. As the Trail unrolled beneath our boots, the wilderness unfolded before our eyes and indeed before all of our senses.

It was along the headwaters of the Penobscot that we first hiked on the Trail in Maine. At this particular time the rains had come to break what had been a drought of considerable severity. The sky was white with overcast, the mountains shrouded in mists that only now and then revealed a portion of a ridge or half a cliff. At this time we still had virtually no idea of the topography, for the haze and mist had been so dense on our arrival that outlines of mountains had been only barely visible, without depth or distance. So we still had not obtained a view of the master eminence of Katahdin, nor of any of its flanking ridges and peaks.

Our walkway lay through a wood where winds of the past had toppled spruce and cedar in assorted directions, throwing some of them together tepee fashion. Logs lay across the trail, and we had to go around, climb over, or squeeze under them—taking care to keep from catching or tearing our packs.

Some logs had been anchored in place so that travelers could cross a tiny stream or bog. Our boots were already muddy, of course, but every log was a help; at least we didn't have to wade. The very wetness rendered these logs as slippery as poles anointed with oil.

We approached a stream that gently poured from a pond a short distance away. Forest debris had floated out from the lake and gathered here in a jam of no small proportions. The familiar white blazes of the Trail had been painted directly on one fallen log after another, and so we hopped—as lumberjacks might—in a haphazard skittering across the poles. You slip and you fall in places like this, there is no other way. You become accustomed to it. You only hope that the final fracture will be mild so that you can hop to the nearest road.

It is almost impossible for us to remember from a distance what the scent of the north woods is like. We have to be there. We cannot capture it on film or tape-record it; we cannot take it with us. There are pine-scented sachets, of course, and balsam soap and candles and incense. But they do not convey the whole. Once away from the woods our olfactory nerves cease transmitting the incredible fragrance of the scene. We remember how it affected us, but we cannot smell it unless we are there.

This woody essence seemed to come to us overwhelmingly, like an anesthetic, as we hiked beyond the log jam. Combined with the quiet and solitude, it seemed to dull our senses. Had we but relaxed our guard, a kind of lassitude could have veiled our march, which up to then had been with spirit and vigor. At the same time, paradoxically, our minds were alert; our eyes and our senses were open to the woodland and all it contained.

More than anything else, the surprises of the dark woods are things that are white. We stopped to find clusters of Indian pipes beneath the spruce, more evidence of the versatile heath family. Tiny white mushrooms grew among the moss, as if the greenery were sprinkled with drops of snow. Leaf lichens festooned the bark and twigs of conifers. In open vales spread reindeer moss, that ubiquitous Cladonia that graces the forest floor almost as thickly and richly as does a wall-to-wall carpet at home.

After fog or rain each needle of fir held at its tip a raindrop that caught the gleam of the sky, as if the limbs were hung with rhinestones.

Suddenly the rattle of a kingfisher and the call of a jay served notice that there were voices in the air. From the trees came the machine-gun chatter of squirrel or chipmunk as a reminder that human walkers, not in possession of prior rights, are merely intruders into another realm. So the Maine woods, under the spell of which we immediately fell, were full of sounds that nearly everywhere compelled us to stop, to look and to listen. No monotonous forest this; it was as busy as a city.

From time to time the trees opened magically upon a view of a pond. By any standard, these make this land as peaceful as any on earth. Framed by spruce boughs, softened by mist, the surface mirroring spires of conifers on the distant shore: this is something for an artist's mind and eye. We saw pondweed and lily pads with their yellow flowers above the shallows. Dragonflies skimmed the water. White-throated sparrows flitted around in witch hazel bushes ashore, or dipped into the water for a bath. Bees gathered honey from wild white clover, and there were yarrow, aster, and the exquisite orange touch-me-not. We never passed a pond in Maine without stopping. The mind and eye, whether of artist or not, are filled to overflowing with the sights and sounds of this land.

We plowed through pondside thickets hip and shoulder high, or paused on blueberry heaths to scoop up handfuls of the ripe fruit. At times we skirted brilliant magenta thistles royally bearing their coronet-like blossoms at eye level.

Thunder seemed to issue from the southwest and the sky grew darker—but we scarcely noticed. Sapsuckers were climbing spruce boles in the dark of the thickets, rabbits were hopping across the trail, and flocks of juncos were chattering in the woods. If we stepped off the trail, we stepped onto a forest floor emblazoned with glossy scarlet bunchberries, with which grew lichen, ferns, moss, oxalis and tiny firs, so thick and luxuriant that if elsewhere created and opened to the public as a garden, an admission would be charged.

There was no hour, no time, no passage of daylight or changing of shadows. We perceived no forward movement of the wooded universe or the universe of time—yet everything was happening. And it was happening at once.

At Little Niagara Falls, on Nesowadnehunk Stream (Sowdy-hunk as the old-timers pronounce it), the scene was one of action and violence. The waters themselves cascaded over boulders and ledges, or plunged against logs caught in the rapids. The trees in the forest bent forward and back in wild agitation under the storm-borne winds. Thunder crashed and echoed in the clouds overhead, clouds that seemed to be spinning and boiling and churning as in a vortex. Far in the distance; seen through the first raindrops that had started pelting down, the dark mountain summits were covered with clouds that raced like leaping white stallions across the ridges.

In half an hour the heaviest of the storm was over, and the sky was cleared with breathtaking suddenness. Only a few veils of diaphanous fog remained in the low places when, late in the afternoon, we came to the edge of a pond. As we broke out of the trees and looked up, there in a scene as beautiful as any we had seen was Katahdin. With all its appurtenances, it rose immensely out of the forest, or more correctly took a great deal of the forest with it. Peak by peak, each of which seemed to have broken through the forest to thrust up its barren core, the range formed a giant amphitheater. Except for scars of open granite, the result of landslides, the forest clothed the lower slopes in an unbroken mass of green, which toward the summit ridges gave way to prominent crags and open boulder fields of enormous extent.

As we watched—as evening slowly came—the surface of the pond grew still. A few clouds appeared on the peak, and as night set in, the mists formed in mid-air, drifted lazily over the top, and vanished.

We sat there for a long time. That wilderness and those moments embodied the spirit of the walker, and the spirit that went into the creation of The Appalachian Trail. Whatever troubles or vexations we might have had all vanished as we contemplated the pond and forest and mountain range that quiet evening. The wonder of man himself, alone of all creatures able to appreciate such scenes, fixed deeply upon our consciousness.

When we left the pond, refreshed in body and mind, we knew of Katahdin what Enos Mills knew of the Rockies: he who feels the spirit of the wild feels also the spirit of human brotherhood.

That night we lay in a lean-to on the Trail, in our *sacs de couchage*, listening to the rumble of thunder in the distance and watching the flashes of lightning growing nearer. Never having experienced a full-scale night storm in Maine, we waited in eager anticipation.

At first, for about two minutes, the rain fell gently and evenly on the shelter roof. Then, with a rise in the wind, the trees overhead spilled their brief accumulation in erratic showers that came down on the roof as if a batch of marbles had been released.

Lightning struck more closely, and we could hear and feel the thunder despite the racket on the roof. The whole scene produced in our minds a singular restfulness, though it was not without a trace of apprehension. After all, here we were on the edge of a stream, which we imagined to be the sole outlet of a vast interior basin—the Katahdin amphitheater—beyond which this storm had formed and through which its gathered waters would pour.

When the cloudburst opened in earnest, we knew in a moment that it was an experience unlike any other. What a pouring of water! What a clatter of marbles! We could not have heard each other talk if we had tried.

Across the front of the lean-to we had hung a tarpaulin on nails that in the past had been driven into logs there, but the tarpaulin did not enclose the opening fully. Through each side burst light from continuous flashes of lightning. The wind, at its peak, forced the trees to yield their watery contents, which poured onto the roof. A waterfall could not have been more deafening.

How much of the roar was from floodwaters rising over the banks of the stream we had no notion. From our experiences in the desert, this could be a matter of life and death; flash floods through arroyos often swept away human lives and possessions.

For what must have been an hour, the storm proceeded without any sign of abatement. It was impossible to imagine how such intensity could be sustained. Lightning flashed closer, and eventually took out a tree (or took out something) within barely a hundred yards of the lean-to.

What a tumult! We could predict precisely what Thoreau and Bartram would have said: "A noble storm!" John Muir, had he been there.

would have rushed from the lean-to in a sort of ecstasy, to feel the wind and rain against his face, to exult beneath the stark white outpourings of light, to hurl himself against the elements.

For a long time after the torrent had tapered off, the trees delivered their floods at the will of the wind. Each drop as it crashed made a sound with a different musical tone. Each had a watery, throaty, vibrating sound, almost identical to that marvelous Central American instrument, the marimba. (We had just heard marimbas, in all their variations, at Chichicastenango and on the shores of Lake Atitlán, in Guatemala, not two weeks before, and this rooftop music had special meaning.)

We cannot say how this concert ended. The last we remember of the storm was another fall of water—and we were sound asleep.

Next morning the sky was gray, the birches and maples still. We emerged from the lean-to expecting to see a roaring, flooded stream tearing away embankments and uprooting trees. But *mirabile dictu*, the stream flowed crystal clear and placid among the granite boulders and beneath the maple boughs that bent down almost to its surface. It was not flooded or roaring; it had not risen much more than an inch. The woods themselves, with their springy turf, had absorbed the rain as they had for centuries. The forest was as peaceful and pleasant as the morning—or the millennium—before.

After breakfast we packed and went on up the Trail toward Katahdin.

Thoreau laid emphasis on that word *up*. As usual, The Appalachian Trail had not been flagged into a devious path of lesser grade. The original pioneers who established the trail up Katahdin went straight to the top. No zigzags, no switchbacks, no U-turns.

It was rough going, like much of the Trail route in Maine. The Appalachian Trail enters the state along the Mahoosuc Range, directly after traversing the crests of the White Mountains. The Mahoosucs are said by many a hiker to be the most beautiful and most rugged section of The Appalachian Trail. Though there are fewer ridges and valleys than in Pennsylvania and Virginia, the Trail trends fairly steadily to

At Jim Whyte's Lookout the authors examine a rock outcrop that has been beveled and polished by glaciers.

The clear mountain waters of Little Wilson Stream cascade into a wilderness swimming pool beside The Appalachian Trail in Maine.

PRECEDING PAGE: Katahdin's Great Basin. The mountain, which in places resembles the Rockies, is one of The Appalachian Trail's most spectacular features.

Little Wilson Falls, of which we see here only the upper half of its 57-foot height, is reached by a side trail that penetrates some of the most remote of the Maine woods.

the northeast, looping over and around some of the most extraordinary mountains in the eastern United States, and passing some of the most scenic lakes.

After crossing Old Speck, in the Mahoosuc Range, third highest mountain in Maine (4,180 feet), the Trail dives to Grafton Notch, a sharp descent of 2,600 feet in a little over one-and-a-half miles. This is good porcupine country, and in fact, Maine still has a fairly stable population of wild animals. The wolf is gone, and so is the caribou that used to roam the northern portions (attempts are being made to reintroduce caribou in the Katahdin region); but moose are fairly well distributed throughout the state, holding their own at approximately three thousand individuals. There are ten times more beaver, and something on the order of two hundred thousand deer, plus bears, fishers, foxes, wildcats, snowshoe hares, and other species surviving from the original fauna.

In this damp and steeply pitching wilderness, the hiker walks and slides on slippery moss that barely clings to the boulders. Make no mistake. It is dangerous walking. It is not for the weak, the unknowing, the unprepared. This is not a tame trail. A hiker needs first-class walking gear and should always be ready to administer first aid. If icy conditions are present, the danger is multiplied.

Straying off the trail has hazards, too. By sliding off a slab and plummeting 600 feet down the face of a precipice, as a friend of ours has done, one gains an excellent view of the lands below, but the view is terribly brief and ends much too abruptly. Our friend survived, and even went back to hike and climb again, but most mortals are not so favored by the gods. The Appalachian Trail and the land through which it passes are, however, safely enjoyed when normal, common-sense precautions are taken. "It is unwise," said Thoreau, "for one to ramble over these mountains at any time, unless he is prepared to move with as much certainty as if he were solving a geometrical problem."

The very magnitude of this land leaves little room for the timid or short-of-vision. To hike through it and become a part of it, to enter what in reality constitutes another world and be changed almost ruthlessly, is to receive something of the essence, perhaps even the immortality, of the land.

Beyond the Mahoosuc Range, the forest-covered islands in Mooselookmeguntic Lake seem to have been carved in conformity to the general outlines of the lake. Into the distance, beyond this exquisite body of water, mountains rise and disappear in fading shades of blue.

Maine has a Saddleback Mountain and a Sugarloaf Mountain here within about ten miles of each other. Sugarloaf, 4,237 feet, is the second highest peak in Maine, and north of it is the handsome Bigelow Range. The views are magnificent and so are the mountains, but the wildness here is disturbed by the encroachment of private developments. "Must every state," the hiker begins to wonder, "have a Sun Valley?"

En route to the Carry Ponds, which nestle eastward in less elevated mountains, the Trail is carpeted almost solidly with moss, dwarf dogwood and oxalis. The latter blooms and arrests the shadows with its cheerful glow, shining out from tangles of logs that lie decaying in vales and hollows. The forest comes all the way to the edge of the Carry Ponds, and then some. Trees have toppled into the shallows. Old bleached logs rest among the giant granite boulders that edge the water. Within the forest, chestnut-sided and black-and-white warblers circulate among the trees; while at the pondside, waxwings sweep out over the water, and even farther out we see a loon (every pond has one, or ought to) diving, surfacing, diving.

This is historic country. The Carry Ponds were named for the innumerable canoe carries necessary in traversing an old Indian route that was established to avoid the "great bend" of the Dead River. Probably the most prodigious and best known "carry" was Benedict Arnold's ill-fated expedition of 1775, which slogged through and around the Carry Ponds on its way to Quebec. Misinformed, poorly provisioned, and using heavy boats hammered out of green wood, Arnold's dwindling forces literally inched their way through the swamps, bogs, lakes and rivers of Maine. The region of the ponds is now known as the Great Carrying Place.

The Kennebec River, its beauty compromised by thousands of floating saw logs, is not what it was in Arnold's day. Passing numerous haul roads and cutover "slash" areas, the hiker finally crosses the Kennebec on a ferry, after which he passes over ledges of andalusite schist and comes to Moxie Pond and Mountain, which John Burroughs described.

As the Trail passes Bald Mountain, Breakneck Ridge and Doughty Hill, it approaches a classic resting place. Many camps and shelters have been passed, but if there were ever a perfect hideaway this side of paradise, it is Little Wilson Campsite.

In all directions is a mixed hardwood forest of maple and such conifers as hemlock, spruce and cedar, with abundant patches of wild raspberry. The forest floor is livened with bright red berries of dwarf dogwood, and the soil is soft and rich and springy, matted coarsely with grass.

Little Wilson has space for pitching several tents, and there are fireplaces and sheltered tables. What perfects the site, however, is the stream itself. A rushing waterfall appears out of the forest about fifty yards away and its foaming water slides over a slatey incline into a deep, wide pool. This pool, overhung by trees and lined with rocky benches and grassy shelves, epitomizes all the wilderness swimming pools there ever were.

At its upper end, the water, fresh in from the sliding fall, runs swiftly. But then it is tamed, though not quite into placidity, and after a while pours out through clefts in the rock and once more bounds away in a singing cascade.

One night at Little Wilson renders camping elsewhere almost anticlimactic. Its solitude, remoteness and simple magnificence are summary characteristics of The Appalachian Trail. Maine has other campsites along the Trail, however, and they are pleasing in their own way. Some are without a stream, some with; some are at the edges of ponds or lakes; most, through the assistance of the Maine Forest Service and private owners, possess the simple elements of wildness which the mountain men and guides and trappers enjoyed so many years ago. Theirs was a rugged land, and today it still retains a great deal of the primitiveness it must have had when the Moosehead Trail was really a trail.

Jim Whyte, a somewhat less than exemplary pioneer, invested his energies in a lurid career of smuggling drugs from Canada. His "lookout," reached by a blue-blazed side trail branching from The Appalachian Trail near Little Wilson Stream, reveals a forested panorama of cliffs and partially barren peaks, with the rails of the Canadian Pacific climbing a slope across the valley. The cabin located here was, until 1929, Whyte's home, and is said to have been a station in the smuggling operations.

Tall spruce with clusters of pendant cones surround the lookout, itself a point of rocks overridden by glacial ice. The upturned ridges of slate were beveled to an almost level surface, on which may be seen abundant grooves and scratches gouged by pebbles or boulders embedded in the ice.

Shoulder-high bracken fern, thickets of young fir and hemlock, wet and grassy bogs—constant plowing, climbing, sloshing—this is the way of the Trail in Maine. En route to Little Wilson Falls (about a mile upstream from the Campsite) the hiker's head gets tangled in cobwebs and he loses his way more times than one. So thickly canopied are parts of the Trail that only spots of sunlight succeed in passing through, which gives the impression that the darkened path is sprinkled with stars. Along this section, it seems as though there are as many kinds and shapes and colors of mushrooms as of flowers.

Down a steep ridge and through heavy underbrush on a side trail we fought our way to the brink of a chasm out of which came boiling spray and a thunderous roar. A wide and powerful waterfall some fifty feet in height, its upper edge enclosed by conifers bent over the stream, plunged down a geometric series of stairsteps carved in solid slate. Earth movements and weather had broken and cracked the slate into curious angular fragments; abstracted on canvas, it would have generated instant notice at a gallery of modern art.

Step after step, leap after leap, Little Wilson Falls, slightly tinged with yellow from its mineral and organic content, plummeted almost out of sight into the narrow gorge. Down there was utter turbulence. The water seethed in a boiling foam past tilted terraces of slate. Moss and fern grew from the cliff wherever a little moisture oozed into a crevice, and where they did not occur, the crustose lichens grew. Limbs of fallen maple clutched the ledge, ready to plunge at any moment into the maelstrom.

We watched water cascade into a narrow gateway, and come up so sharply against a corner beyond that a geyser five feet high burst out of the foam. Farther on, the river tumbled from ledge to ledge and cauldron to cauldron until it vanished from sight. It was a cataract to remember— hidden, remote, spectacular; Thoreau, had he been there, would almost surely have called it a noble piece of nature.

And now, at its northern end, The Appalachian Trail continued the familiar winding and dipping that characterizes it through the wild lake lands of Maine. At Katahdin Stream Campground, signs advised that only 5 miles of Trail remained.

But what a 5 miles!

As we rose higher, the stream rose too, more often heard than seen, tumbling past in a continuous roar through the tangle of beech and birch and maple.

We passed a freshly broken surface of granite, base rock of these ancient mountains. The grains were coarse and handsome, almost a pegmatite in texture. Feldspar crystals added a touch of pink, but the quartz was perfectly clear. All this produced a curious trail pavement of "graphic granite," so called because the intergrown minerals resemble written records of ancient civilizations.

Long before there were interstate highways, almost before there were automobiles, a man named Percival Baxter recognized that the beauty of the Katahdin region would one day be severely encroached upon if someone didn't preserve it while there still was time. Baxter served five terms in the Maine legislature and two terms as Governor, and during this period sought to make his colleagues as keenly aware of Maine's wild beauty as he was. For various reasons, however, they did not feel that the time had come, and all attempts to preserve the region failed.

Baxter stepped down from the governorship in 1925, but knew that something had to be done to conserve the scenic crown jewel of the northern woods. He then decided to use his own funds. In 1930 he purchased 6,690 acres, including most of the summit of Katahdin, and turned it over to the state, stipulating that the land be held as a wildlife sanctuary and used as a public forest, park and recreation area.

In addition to this, Baxter continued efforts to save the region, and his later contributions raised the size of the preserve to 201,018 acres. In 1931 the Maine legislature voted to name it Baxter State Park. The summit was named Baxter Peak. And so it is today.

The hiker contemplates with due respect this work of Baxter, and finds himself again in debt to a man, and men, of vision. On his own he feels possessed of an obligation to keep the forest clean, leave only footprints, and fight to save endangered areas elsewhere.

"Man is born to die," said Baxter, whose words are now engraved on a plaque at the Katahdin Stream Campground. "His works are short lived. Buildings crumble, monuments decay, wealth vanishes. But Katahdin in all its glory forever shall remain the mountain of the people of Maine."

Soon the foothills are left behind and the ascent becomes nearly vertical. Katahdin Stream is now almost a single cascade, interrupted only by boulders on the slope. In it lie colorful pebbles of granite, slate, andesite and a host of other rock varieties—an excellent illustration of the igneous geology of the mountain.

The path is strewn with tree roots crossing in all directions. Sand having formed a level layer between successive levels of roots contributes to the making of a stairway. But not for long. At other times the steps are only rocks, and the great ascent continues.

The path becomes more of a test of climbing than of hiking. After Katahdin Stream Falls, a picturesque sheet of white water plummeting among the gray rocks, the Trail pitches even more sharply, root after root, rock after rock, step after step.

The forest begins to thin out; the trees are smaller; there are dead or dying trees in greater abundance. Then, for a while, the trees close in again and so do the clouds. It is a true cloud forest, and not without life, for a hiker may discern a grouse in the rocky patches, or see kinglets and Canada and black-poll warblers among the branches.

The steps of boulders have become large enough for Paul Bunyan himself—who, to hear people in these parts tell it, was born in Argyle, Maine, and only after bad luck here, headed west to log off South Dakota (*not* Minnesota) and accomplish other prodigious feats. According to the Maine version of the story, Bunyan died at the age of ninety-one and his body was brought back to be buried along the West Branch in a casket made of molasses hogsheads.

If these boulders were right for Paul Bunyan, they are far too big for ordinary mortals, and so the hiker clambers and pulls and clings as best he can. From here on up, the Trail becomes an obstacle course as much as anything else, and at last breaks out of the trees onto open boulder fields.

"I entered within the skirts of the cloud which seemed forever drifting over the summit," said Thoreau of his Katahdin climb, "and yet would never be gone, but was generated out of that pure air as fast as it flowed away; and when, a quarter of a mile farther, I reached the summit of the ridge, which those who have seen it in clearer weather say is about five miles long, and contains a thousand acres of table-land, I was deep within the hostile ranks of clouds, and all objects were obscured by them. Now the wind would blow me out a yard of clear sunlight, wherein I stood; then a gray, dawning light was all it could accomplish, the cloud-line ever rising and falling with the wind's intensity. Sometimes it seemed as if the summit would be cleared in a few moments, and smile in sunshine; but what was gained on one side was lost on another. It was like sitting in a chimney and waiting for the smoke to blow away. It was, in fact, a cloud factory—these were the cloud-works, and the wind turned them off done from the cool, bare rocks. Occasionally, when the windy columns broke in to me, I caught sight of a dark, damp crag to the right or left; the mist driving ceaselessly between it and me. It reminded me of the creations of the old epic and dramatic poets, of Atlas, Vulcan, the Cyclops, and Prometheus. Such was Caucasus and the rock where Prometheus was bound. Aeschylus had no doubt visited such scenery as this. It was vast, Titanic, and such as man never inhabits. . . ."

At a simple bronze registration cylinder on this dramatic summit, 5,267 feet above sea level, The Appalachian Trail comes to an end. From here, clouds permitting, the deep north woods spread out in every direction, spotted with lakes, interrupted by barren ridges, a land as close to original wilderness as the laws and works of men allow.

Here on top of the world—a hiker's own world in more ways than one—the mind lifts up, as Plato would have said, into the stars. On a lonely peak, to lonely men, the achievement of this mountain and this Trail provide, as much as anywhere else, that "planetary feeling" which once urged a man to dream of the Trail, and which the Trail now gives to other men.

It is a good feeling. When the hiker starts down, he carries that feeling with him, and for a long, long time it stays with him. He has been on the throne of the gods and is content.

10

I love not Man the less, but Nature more,
From these our interviews. . . .

Lord Byron

I Wonder As I Wander

"I looked across the gulches and valleys of the landscape far away from Katahdin and saw the mirror surfaces of a hundred or more lakes in vast stretches of mountains. Not another scene like it elsewhere on the Trail or elsewhere on earth. So ended the Trail in beauty, grandeur, and perfection; just as every trail, including the trail of life, should end."

Thus wrote a hiker after a full-length summer hike of The Appalachian Trail. What changes this wild and simple trail makes in a person! He has time he never had before; time to ponder, time for meditation. In certain circles, this word has come to rest in bad repute. It seems almost a word of curious meaning from another language. In our rapidly spinning world we rarely have time on our hands, and when we do—what is this thing called meditation?

"Not only do people in a democratic society have difficulty meditating," said Alexis de Tocqueville, writing about American democracy, "they do not care for it by nature. Democracy and its institutions drive people to incessant activity. The frame of mind that favors activity does not always encourage thinking. Generally, quick decisions and superficial notions are preferred where people are wrapped up in their work, while deep, circumspect intellectual pursuits are underrated. People are so much involved in their work that there is little time left for meditation. They pursue their business with such ardor that thoughts cannot set them afire."

Once on the Trail, however, all that is over. There are bright days when the sun pours its energy into the leaves, and the hiker, watching this, grows as the leaf grows, expanding in time and space and comprehension. He walks among the trees, he becomes a part of this natural world, he feels its sadness and its joy, its rhythmic sense of beauty and power and eternity, and its endless inspiration. He walks among the giants of the world, for he walks in epic strides himself, and his troubles fall a step or two behind. It is then that he is in tune with the wilderness.

"Everything familiar and trite and tired is rolled up behind you some place," wrote Alberta Pierson Hannum. "The world is new and raw and beautiful and there isn't a mistake in it. You have come eagerly, needing this. You thought you had remembered. But you find you had forgotten. You had forgotten the power, the power and the peace, the uselessness of petty things. The freedom!"

The delicious freedom to let your mind wander—it is a freedom to be cherished. Everything is equal on the Trail: past and present, young and old, bitter and sweet, far and near. Each step is another milestone into this never-never land where the brain, relaxed, plays tricks of the oddest kind.

Move down to the creek. Step carefully, wary of moss. Cross the stones. Duck under a birch limb—stop for a moment and listen. No moose in there. No fox or raccoon or hare. There was a loon back awhile; keep listening for another. Now up the trail through more birch. Keep those legs going. Forget the fatigue. Forget the soreness in the back muscles. Ignore the shoulder pains from the pack. Just keep going on. . . .

There is no limit but the boiling point of our own ennui, it has been written, and that implacable master, time. There are no conventions. Who, for example, would hike on The Appalachian Trail in winter? Some persons do, the hardy and well-equipped. With the temperature approaching zero and the promise of snow flurries—what a glorious time to get going! And are peaks climbed at this time of year? Let a witness speak:

"It was about zero, the wind was blowing and it was snowing lightly. When I walked out onto the windswept summit, it seemed almost as if I had emerged on another planet. All around me was nothing but white wilderness, with no sign of lake or habitation. The wind moaned eerily, as if resenting any intrusion. The top of the mountain looked as if a giant had sliced the top off, and left the tracks of time behind. The trees were coated with snow and rime, and as they are stunted and one-sided for a moment it seemed to me as if the world was tilting. I only wish that I could have caught up the scene and spread it out here for you. If ever you have the opportunity to climb a mountain in the winter, do it, by all means. You will come down seeing civilization with a new eye, and have a new appreciation for the imagination and courage and strength which our forefathers had to conquer this land of ours."

And so The Appalachian Trail has its own special meaning to each person who travels along it. If at first the hiker does not understand the language of the whispering pines or the murmuring of the stream, this learning will almost surely come in time. Once the barrier against solitude is overcome, the hiker will one day realize that walking is a form of selective concentration, and with that his thoughts wait only to be ignited.

"I've had many extended periods with the dual advantage of isolation and solitude in the mountains," wrote a hiking veteran of more than two thousand miles on the A.T. "These experiences brought about a greater comprehension of my relationship with Nature, and a greater feeling of being part of it; in addition they gave me a greater ability to judge the true value of things, and a greater ability to derive pleasure from every aspect of my natural surroundings. Continually, indeed almost daily, I think back on the pleasures that I've had on the Trail and the teachings that it has imparted to me, and how those pleasures and teachings have given me happiness and a greater understanding of how to bring fullness and richness to my life."

Psychologists say that whatever is can be measured, but there are times when they admit that the tools for measuring some things have not been perfected. The inspiration of the wilderness is one; it can be real and abstract all at once. We are left with the poet to sum up the essence for us and to bring out the poetry within ourselves.

Miss Hannum wrote: "When the spirit is world-heavy, weighed down with all the mistakes and confusions and sorrows and humiliations that can come in the frail time of humans, it is like promise to stand in a morning when the near hills are dark with the feel of rain, but away off the far ones are in a lighted mist. It is beautiful and good over there, and clean and simple. It is more positive than solace. The very promise that the heart can be light again, lets you turn, and go onward. . . ."

The Appalachian Trail does something to a person—and for him. It gives him that "planetary feeling," and a new collection of independent thoughts which are not to be gained solely from reading, talking, writing or attending lectures. He understands the language of the Trail, and hence of nature. He understands himself.

One hiker who walked the entire Trail in a summer was looked upon with awe by friends and acquaintances. Someone predicted that he would get his picture in the paper. "Sure enough I did," he said later, "but I think the best picture I got of myself was on a beautiful day last year from Mt. Lafayette in the White Mountains. As I looked down and out, tracing the path I followed, I saw myself traveling this path as small as the smallest creature, just a speck of dust on the vastness before me, and this vastness just a small speck in the vastness of the universe."

No single formula for success exists in matters so fundamental and yet so abstract. On the wilderness trail we may wonder as we wander, sorting out the elements of meditation and pleasure. And whatever else it may produce in the minds of men, The Appalachian Trail will always be, God and the public willing, a high road to paradise where we may walk and dream to our heart's content.

Appendix I

THE APPALACHIAN TRAIL CONFERENCE

Membership in the Appalachian Trail Conference consists of four classes: Class A, clubs which maintain specific portions of The Appalachian Trail; Class B, clubs which support, by other means, The Appalachian Trail project; Class C, public officials (Federal and State) who have charge of areas through which the Trail passes and who maintain the Trail therein, and persons maintaining in an individual capacity certain designated portions of the Trail; and Class D, individual members. The Conference encourages support from persons interested in the Trail. For information, contact one of the organizations listed below, or The Appalachian Trail Conference, Box 236, Harpers Ferry, West Virginia 25425.

A. Organizations maintaining sections of the Trail
   1. Georgia Appalachian Trail Club, Box 654, Atlanta, Georgia 30301
   2. Nantahala Hiking Club, Franklin, North Carolina 28734
   3. Smoky Mountains Hiking Club, Box 1454, Knoxville, Tennessee 37901
   4. Carolina Mountain Club, Asheville, North Carolina
   5. Tennessee Eastman Hiking Club, B-54-D Tennessee Eastman Company, Kingsport, Tennessee 37662
   6. Mount Rogers Appalachian Trail Club, Abingdon, Virginia 24210
   7. Piedmont Appalachian Trail Hikers, Greensboro, South Carolina
   8. Roanoke Appalachian Trail Club, Roanoke, Virginia 24012
   9. Natural Bridge Appalachian Trail Club, Lynchburg, Virginia 24505
   10. Shenandoah-Rockfish Appalachian Trail Club, Charlottesville, Virginia, and Waynesboro, Virginia

11. Potomac Appalachian Trail Club, 1718 N Street N.W., Washington, D.C. 20036
12. Mountain Club of Maryland, Baltimore, Maryland
13. Susquehanna Appalachian Trail Club, Harrisburg, Pennsylvania 17103
14. Brandywine Valley Outing Club, Wilmington, Delaware 19803
15. Lancaster Hiking Club, Lancaster, Pennsylvania 17603
16. Allentown Hiking Club, Allentown, Pennsylvania 18102
17. Blue Mountain Eagle Climbing Club, Reading, Pennsylvania 19603
18. Delaware Valley Chapter, Appalachian Mountain Club, Philadelphia, Pennsylvania
19. Philadelphia Trail Club, Philadelphia, Pennsylvania
20. Back to Nature Hiking Club, Philadelphia, Pennsylvania
21. Alpha Phi Omega, Lafayette College, College Station, Easton, Pennsylvania
22. Delaware Water Gap, Chamber of Commerce, Delaware Water Gap, Pennsylvania 18327
23. New York - New Jersey Trail Conference, G.P.O. Box 2250, New York, New York 10001
    a. New York Chapter, Appalachian Mountain Club
    b. Westchester Trails Association
    c. Woodland Trail Walkers
    d. New York Section, Green Mountain Club
    e. Adirondack Mountain Club
    f. Ramapo Ramblers
    g. Girl Mariners
    h. Wilderness Club
    i. Union County Hiking Club
    j. New York Ramblers
    k. Sierra Club, Atlantic Chapter
    l. Senior Scout Troop 43, Boy Scouts of America
    m. Orange Mountain Council, Boy Scouts of America
    n. Torrey Botanical Club
    o. Robert Treat Council, Boy Scouts of America
24. Connecticut Chapter, Appalachian Mountain Club, Cheshire, Connecticut 06410
25. Berkshire Chapter, Appalachian Mountain Club, Springfield, Massachusetts 01118
26. Metawampe Club, Amherst, Massachusetts 01002
27. Mount Greylock Ski Club, Pittsfield, Massachusetts 01201
28. Green Mountain Club, 108 Merchants Row, Rutland, Vermont 05701

29. Dartmouth Outing Club, Robinson Hall, Hanover, New Hampshire 03755

30. Appalachian Mountain Club, 5 Joy Street, Boston, Massachusetts 02108

31. Maine Appalachian Trail Club, Kents Hill, Maine 04349
    a. Camp Allagash, Greenville, Maine 04441
    b. Narragansett Chapter, Appalachian Mountain Club, Riverside, Rhode Island 02915
    c. Colby Woodsmens Club, Colby College, Waterville, Maine 04901
    d. Piscataquis County Fish and Game Association, Monson, Maine 04464
    e. Future Farmers of America, Foxcroft Academy, Dover-Foxcroft, Maine 04426
    f. University of Maine Outing Club, Orono, Maine 04473
    g. Pine Island Camp, Belgrade Lakes, Maine 04918
    h. Maine Trail Trotters, Winthrop, Maine 04364
    i. Boy Scout Troop 104, Winthrop, Maine 04364
    j. Portland Chapter, Appalachian Mountain Club, Portland, Maine 04101
    k. Wilton Outing Club, Wilton, Maine 04294
    l. Franklin County Fish & Game Club, Dryden, Maine 04225
    m. Bates Outing Club, Lewiston, Maine 04240

B. Organizations not maintaining sections of the Trail but contributing support
    1. Middle Georgia Girl Scout Council, Macon, Georgia 31201
    2. Appalachian Girl Scout Council, Johnson City, Tennessee 37601
    3. Terrapin Ski Club, College Park, Maryland 20740
    4. Maryland Appalachian Trail Club, Hagerstown, Maryland 21740
    5. Wanderbirds Hiking Club, Washington, D.C.
    6. Wilmington Trail Club, Wilmington, Delaware 19899
    7. Blue Mountain Wilderness Park Association, Reading, Pennsylvania 19603
    8. Horse-Shoe Trail Club, Ardmore, Pennsylvania 19003
    9. Keystone Trails Association, Concordsville, Pennsylvania 19331
    10. Lebanon Valley Hiking Club, Lebanon, Pennsylvania 17042
    11. Interstate Hiking Club, Bloomfield, New Jersey 07003
    12. Taconic Hiking Club, Cohoes, New York 12047
    13. Tramp and Trail Club of New York

14. New York City Troop 527, Boy Scouts of America
15. Connecticut Park and Forest Association, 15 Lewis Street, Hartford, Connecticut 06103
16. New England Trail Conference, Ashfield, Massachusetts 01330

C. Ex-Officio Members (officials having supervision over public lands traversed by the Trail)
1. Chief Forester, Forest Service, United States Department of Agriculture, Washington, D.C. 20250
2. Regional Forester, Region 7, Forest Service, Philadelphia, Pennsylvania 19101
3. Regional Forester, Region 8, Forest Service, Atlanta, Georgia 30301
4. Supervisor, White Mountain National Forest, Laconia, New Hampshire 03246
5. Supervisor, Green Mountain National Forest, Rutland, Vermont 05702
6. Supervisor, George Washington National Forest, Harrisonburg, Virginia 22801
7. Supervisor, Jefferson National Forest, Roanoke, Virginia 24101
8. Supervisor, Cherokee National Forest, Cleveland, Tennessee 37312
9. Supervisor, North Carolina National Forests, Asheville, North Carolina 28801
10. Supervisor, Chattahoochee National Forest, Gainesville, Georgia
11. Director, National Park Service, United States Department of the Interior, Washington, D.C. 20240
12. Superintendent, Shenandoah National Park, Luray, Virginia 22835
13. Superintendent, Blue Ridge Parkway, Asheville, North Carolina 28807.
14. Superintendent, Great Smoky Mountains National Park, Gatlinburg, Tennessee 37738
15. State Forester, Augusta, Maine 04330
16. Supervisor, Baxter State Park, Togue Ponds, Millinocket, Maine 04462
17. State Forester, Forestry and Recreation Department, Concord, New Hampshire 03301
18. Chairman, Vermont Department of Conservation and Development, Barre, Vermont 05641
19. State Forester, Montpelier, Vermont 05602
20. Commissioner of Conservation, Boston, Massachusetts 02101
21. Chairman, Mount Greylock Commission, Pittsfield, Massachusetts
22. Forester, October Mountain Forest, Lenox, Massachusetts 01240

23. Forester, Beartown and East Mountain State Forests, Great Barrington, Massachusetts 01230
24. Chairman, Mount Everett Reservation Commission, Great Barrington, Massachusetts 01230
25. Chairman, State Park and Forest Commission, Hartford, Connecticut
26. State Forester, Hartford, Connecticut 06101
27. Director of State Parks, New York Conservation Department, Albany, New York 12201
28. Chairman, Taconic Park Commission, Staatsburg, New York 12580
29. Superintendent, Palisades Interstate Park, Bear Mountain, New York 10911
30. Chairman, Fahnestock State Park Commission, Cold Spring, New York 10516
31. State Forester, Trenton, New Jersey 08625
32. Superintendent, High Point State Park, New Jersey
33. Superintendent, Stokes State Forest, Branchville, New Jersey 07826
34. Secretary, Department of Forests and Waters, Harrisburg, Pennsylvania 17120
35. Executive Director, Pennsylvania Game Commission, Harrisburg, Pennsylvania 17120
36. Forester, Michaux State Forest, Fayetteville, Pennsylvania 17222
37. State Forester, Annapolis, Maryland 21401
38. Director, State Forests and Parks, Annapolis, Maryland 21401
39. Director of Conservation, Charleston, West Virginia 25321
40. Director of Conservation, Richmond, Virginia 23201
41. State Forester, University, Virginia
42. Commissioner, Department of Conservation, Nashville, Tennessee 37202
43. Superintendent of State Parks, Department of Conservation and Development, Raleigh, North Carolina 27601
44. Director of State Parks, Atlanta, Georgia 30302

D. Dues-paying Individual Members

Appendix II

PUBLICATIONS AVAILABLE FROM
THE APPALACHIAN TRAIL CONFERENCE
Box 236
Harpers Ferry, West Virginia 25425

The Appalachian Trail Conference is an amateur recreational project. Its activities are on a volunteer basis, the contribution of those who are interested in the Trail project. The Conference is composed of individuals, outing clubs and organizations which support the Trail project. Membership is available for individuals, who receive publications issued by the Conference during the period of their membership (except guidebooks) and *Appalachian Trailway News*. This type of membership affords individuals an opportunity to maintain close contact with and to support the Appalachian Trail project. Further information on membership is available from the Conference at its address shown on page 162.

The Appalachian Trail Conference, as a volunteer organization, is supported by contributions and by receipts from the sale of its publications, which are priced at little more than the cost of printing and mailing. By carefully noting the list of publications, you should find a source of information that will deal with your special interest in The Appalachian Trail.

The entire Trail is described in detail by a series of guidebooks that contain much information that may be needed by the Trail traveler. Other publications treat of the history of the Trail, the system employed in its marking, equipment, camping techniques, lean-to construction, preparation of guidebooks, and other related matters. If you have had no previous experience on the Appalachian Trail or in trail travel, you should find useful A.T.C. Publication No. 15, *Suggestions for Appalachian Trail Users*. This publication was prepared in response to numerous inquiries received over a course of years by the Conference, and will furnish the answers to a wide variety of questions.

If you are primarily interested in the history of The Appalachian Trail,

167

you will find the Conference's Publication No. 5, *The Appalachian Trail,* a thorough statement. This publication also details the route of the Trail, lists the maintaining organizations, sets forth its Constitution, and reprints The Appalachian Trailway Agreement.

A subscription to *Appalachian Trailway News* will keep you informed of important developments along or affecting the Trail, new publications, lightweight hiking and camping equipment, and other matters pertaining to the Trail. This is issued three times a year.

The Trail Guides vary in price generally from $2 to $3 each, but since prices are subject to change, an up-to-date list of publications should be obtained from the Conference.

General Publications

The prices of the following pamphlets are all well under a dollar.

The Appalachian Trail, Publication No. 17. (Contains brief history of the Trail and a description of the route, including map; organization of and membership in the Appalachian Trail Conference; complete list of publications for sale by the Conference.)

The Appalachian Trail, Publication No. 5. (Contains history of the Appalachian Trail, list of trail-maintaining organizations, route of the trail, Conference Constitution, Appalachian Trailway Agreement, and Bibliography.)

Suggestions for Appalachian Trail Users. (Includes information on trip planning, accommodations, precautions, maps, equipment, clothing and food.)

Lightweight Equipment for Hiking, Camping and Mountaineering. (Tells what to buy, and where, and how much it will cost.)

Trail Manual for the Appalachian Trail. (Includes standards, techniques for trail-clearing, tools, marking, sign-making, how to lay out and build a new trail, and information on where to procure trail-maintaining equipment.)

Trail Guides

Guide to The Appalachian Trail in the Great Smokies, the Nantahalas, and Georgia.

Guide to The Appalachian Trail in Tennessee and North Carolina: Cherokee, Pisgah, and Great Smokies.

Guide to The Appalachian Trail in Central and Southwestern Virginia.

Guide to Trails in the Shenandoah National Park: The Appalachian Trail
and Side Trails.

Guide to The Appalachian Trail: Susquehanna River to the Shenandoah
National Park.

Guide to The Appalachian Trail: From the Connecticut-New York State
Line to the Susquehanna River, Pennsylvania.

Guide to The Appalachian Trail in Massachusetts and Connecticut.

Guide to The Appalachian Trail in New Hampshire and Vermont.

Guide to The Appalachian Trail in Maine.

Katahdin Section of Guide to The Appalachian Trail in Maine.

Appendix III

HIKING SUPPLIES AND EQUIPMENT
and Where to Get Them

The newcomer faces a bewildering unknown in regard to what to take on an extended hike. If he does not take enough, he can spend some thoroughly uncomfortable days or hours on the trail. If he plays it safe and takes too much, he is overburdened unnecessarily, and that is not very pleasant either.

To have enough, without being overburdened, the hiker should plan his trip as carefully as possible, and preferably weeks in advance. We have always found it helpful before each trip to assess our needs literally from head to foot, and to pack according to the number of hiking hours or days.

Starting at the head, we decide on whether to wear a hat. Usually we don't, but in cold weather, a warm hat with ear flaps is often desirable. Sunglasses we find helpful; in thick forests they can be removed and placed in the shirt pocket, but out on open slopes the rocks and snow are bright. Sunglasses should always be carried in some kind of protective case. Tinted goggles, if comfortable, are quite satisfactory.

Around the neck we carry binoculars or a camera or both. If they clank together at times, that is the price to pay for having them ready for instant use. In more than 30 years of hiking we have rarely, if ever, embarked upon a trail trip without camera and binoculars; it is something one gets used to. With the new advances in transistors and miniaturization of electronic circuits, one might also take a tape recorder—at the risk of being overburdened and looking like a gadget display rack. Nevertheless, some of our happiest hours have been spent in recording sounds of the wild, adding to the depth of our perception of the wild environment. This is at least something to be considered when seeking ways to add variety and enjoyment to a woods walk; perhaps it could be done in the form of a special hike or two just for recording purposes, most profitably in springtime.

Our packsacks have some standard items that remain there all the time and are more or less ready to go at a moment's notice. These consist of three deerskin bags. One contains emergency food. One contains first-aid equipment and miscellaneous medical supplies. The third contains sundries that we like to have along for convenience or survival: matches, maps, mosquito repellent, compass, small mirror for signaling purposes, extra handkerchief, sun lotion, soap, toilet paper, can opener, and folding cup. Extra socks are carried as a matter of course. Then, by option, we add extra film, guidebooks, and finally the food and other equipment for each specific trip. Many years ago we became addicted to dried peaches, which we load into our packs as heavily as we can bear. They are delicious and nutritious at any time, and especially when pangs of hunger begin to appear.

Depending on the length and location of the hike, attention should be given to taking a canteen. Consult the Trail Guide for spring sites, but take some water just in case the springs are dry or destroyed. Watery fruits such as apples and oranges are excellent for adding to the intake of fluids.

A high-riding pack with a good center of gravity suits us best (see page 73) but on short hikes we prefer a side-riding pack hanging from one shoulder. It has the advantage of permitting easy access to the contents of the pack, and we find no serious objection to the imbalance that may result. We insist on good quality packs, preferably with leather bottoms. It is a waste of time and a source of unnecessary exasperation to settle for poorly designed or manufactured equipment for hiking.

Pencil and note pad are carried either in this side pack or in a shirt pocket. On The Appalachian Trail a Trail Guide is either carried in the pack, or in the hand, or consigned to one of the boys—who is designated "navigator."

A cotton undershirt and cotton shirt have always suited us, with a denim jacket in cool autumn days, and a lightweight quilted jacket in winter. A special advantage is gained from insulated or quilted underwear, which we have found superior to thermal-knit apparel. Insulated wear is a trifle more bulky beneath the outer garments, but it is comfortable and does not bind, is reliably warm, and replaces the need for a heavy outer jacket. In fact, it can double as an outer jacket. Where especially sharp drops in temperature are possible, we carry wool scarves. And when rain gear is desired, we prefer rubberized nylon with a shoulder cape (be prepared to spend $30 or more for all this) and a sou'wester hat packed permanently with the raincoat.

We also belong to the school that prefers full-length trousers—slacks for women—and are not particularly disturbed by excessive body heat that might be trapped around the legs. With the lower extremities reasonably well protected, we can give more attention to observations along the trail.

In the trouser pockets are the usual items: knife, wallet with money and identification, handkerchief and keys.

When it comes to footwear, there must be absolutely no stinting on quality, comfort and safety. A little experimenting will determine which combination of socks is most comfortable (see page 69). Shoes must be durable but soft. We have found over the years that a pair of shoes costing about $30 has more than three times the life expectancy of a pair of shoes costing $10 and there is a world of difference in comfort. Moreover, every time you buy a pair of lesser quality shoes you must break them in, a sometimes painful process. Our experience has been that if higher quality shoes are properly fitted in the first place, break-in time is minimal—and the comfort is enduring. Padded quarters and tongue add to the comfort. Lug soles, as far as we are concerned, are essential; they offer good traction during slick-rock hiking and simply grip better during any kind of climbing or walking. Both men's and women's styles are available. If you must use leather shoes, be wary of slipping on rocks and pine needles.

There is usually little trouble in preparing children for hiking, since they are already more or less outfitted for an active life. Small packs are available for them to carry, and they appreciate the responsibility of helping to carry food supplies or survival gear. Even infants can go on a hike. We have taken them with and without an infant carrier, and can most heartily recommend that parents strap on an infant carrier. There are several styles available, with such names as Kiddie Carrier, Kiddie Pack, and Hike-a-poose. The point is: take the kids along—everyone should enjoy the fun!

On longer hikes, the complexity of equipment increases, and so does the need for careful preplanning. Among other things, the hiker must consider pack frame, tent, sleeping gear, and larger amounts of food.

Fortunately there is a made-to-order source of information, a booklet called Lightweight Equipment for Hiking, Camping, and Mountaineering, published by the Potomac Appalachian Trail Club, and available from the Club or the Appalachian Trail Conference (See Appendix II). Early editions of this bulletin, dating from 1931, were written primarily for the use of club members in the Blue Ridge and Alleghenies. But as the extent and territory of hiking increased, the booklet, prepared by the Camping Equipment Committee of the Potomac Appalachian Trail Club, changed to meet the needs, and now is widely used by hikers in western states and even in countries other than the U.S.A. Still, it is designed especially for the hiker along The Appalachian Trail, and therein lies its major value. Each of the listed items has been tested or examined, and only professionally acceptable items are included. Quality is stressed over cost, but there are suggestions specifically for the beginning backpacker. The booklet lists articles, weights, suppliers and costs, and gives helpful hints on equipping yourself for trail travel.

From coast to coast there are commercial firms offering hiking and camping equipment for sale, and, in some places, for rent. A good place to look is in the yellow pages of the telephone directory, under "Camping Equipment & Supplies." General-merchandise and mail-order catalogs, such as Sears Roebuck and Montgomery Ward, contain a good variety of equipment.

For more comprehensive and specialized suppliers, one should consult up-to-date advertising listings in such periodicals as *Appalachia*, published by the Appalachian Mountain Club, 5 Joy Street, Boston, Massachusetts 02108. Some suppliers publish excellent catalogs in which a hiker can choose from a wide range of equipment offered. Two firms with good catalogs are L. L. Bean, Inc., Freeport, Maine 04032; and Corcoran, Inc., Stoughton, Massachusetts 02072.

As for concentrated, dehydrated, and freeze-dried foods, lists and catalogs can be obtained from distributors such as Chuck Wagon Foods, 176 Oak Street, Newton, Massachusetts 02164; and Stow-A-Way Products Co., Inc., 103 Ripley Road, Cohasset, Massachusetts 02025.

Hikers planning to use The Appalachian Trail should be aware that special backcountry permits and sometimes camping fees are required along certain sections of the Trail. These permits and fees are in effect where the Trail crosses certain popular recreation areas administered by the National Park Service and the U.S. Forest Service. Detailed information may be obtained by writing to the following: Superintendent, Great Smoky Mountains National Park, Gatlinburg, Tennessee 37738; Superintendent, Shenandoah National Park, Luray, Virginia 22835; Supervisor, Green Mountain National Forest, Rutland, Vermont 05701; and Supervisor, White Mountain National Forest, Laconia, New Hampshire 03246.

Bibliography

Adams, Elmer C., *Walking in the Clouds*, 1939, Arnold-Powers, Inc., Detroit, Mich.

Appalachian Mountain Club, *In the Hudson Highlands*, 1945, Appalachian Mountain Club, New York, N.Y.

————, *The A.M.C. White Mountain Guide: A Guide to Trails in the Mountains of New Hampshire*, latest edition, Appalachian Mountain Club, Boston, Mass.

————, *Mountain Flowers of New England*, 1964, Appalachian Mountain Club, Boston, Mass.

Appalachian Trail Conference, Guides and various publications, see Appendix for list.

Ayres, Harral, *The Great Trail of New England*, 1940, Meadow Publ. Co., Boston, Mass.

Billings, Marland P., and others, *The Geology of the Mt. Washington Quadrangle, New Hampshire*, 1946, State Planning and Development Commission, Concord, N.H.

Bowles, Ella Shannon, *Let Me Show You New Hampshire*, 1938, Alfred A. Knopf, Inc., New York, N.Y.

Bowman, Elizabeth Skaggs, *Land of High Horizons*, 1938, Southern Publishers, Inc., Kingsport, Tenn.

Brooks, Maurice, *The Appalachians*, 1965, Houghton Mifflin Co., Boston, Mass.

Broun, Maurice, *Hawks Aloft, the Story of Hawk Mountain*, 1949, Dodd, Mead Co., New York, N.Y.

Bureau of Outdoor Recreation, *Trails for America*, 1966, U.S. Government Printing Office, Washington, D.C.

Burt, F. Allen, *The Story of Mount Washington*, 1960, Dartmouth Publications, Hanover, N.H.

Campbell, Carlos C., *Birth of a National Park in the Great Smoky Mountains*, 1960, Univ. of Tennessee Press, Knoxville, Tenn.

Connecticut Forest and Park Association, *Connecticut Walk Book*, latest edition, Connecticut Forest and Park Association, New Haven, Conn.

Coolidge, P. T., *History of the Maine Woods*, 1963, Furbush-Roberts Printing Co., Bangor, Maine.

Crane, Charles Edward, *Let Me Show You Vermont*, 1937, Alfred A. Knopf, Inc., New York, N.Y.

Douglas, William O., *My Wilderness: East to Katahdin*, 1961, Doubleday & Company, Inc., Garden City, N.Y.

Faris, John T., *Roaming the Eastern Mountains*, 1932, Farrar & Rinehart, Inc., New York, N.Y.

————, *Seeing the Eastern States*, 1922, J. B. Lippincott Co., Philadelphia, Pa.

Fernald, Merritt, and Alfred Kinsey, *Edible Wild Plants of Eastern North America*, 1958, Harper & Bros., New York, N.Y.

Frome, Michael, *Whose Woods These Are: The Story of the National Forests*, 1962, Doubleday & Co., Inc., Garden City, N.Y.

————, *Strangers in High Places*, 1966, Doubleday & Company, Inc., Garden City N.Y.

Harper, Francis, *The Travels of William Bartram, Naturalist's Edition*, 1958, Yale University Press, New Haven, Conn.

Hulbert, Archer B., *Indian Thoroughfares*, 1902, Arthur H. Clark, Cleveland, Ohio.

Hunt, Richard A., *White Mountain Holidays*, 1941, Falmouth Publ. House, Portland, Maine.

Jefferson, Thomas, *Notes on the State of Virginia*, 1861, H. W. Derby, New York, N.Y.; published in paperback in 1964 by Harper & Row, Publishers, New York, N.Y.

Kephart, Horace, *Our Southern Highlanders*, 1941, The Macmillan Company, New York, N.Y.

Kilbourne, Frederick W., *Chronicles of the White Mountains*, 1916, Houghton Mifflin Co., Boston, Mass.

Lee, W. Storrs, and others, *Footpath in the Wilderness*, 1941, Middlebury College Press, Middlebury, Vt.

————, *The Green Mountains of Vermont*, 1955, Henry Holt & Co., New York, N.Y.

Lunt, Dudley Cammett, *The Woods and the Sea: Wilderness and Seacoast Adventures in the State of Maine*, 1965, Alfred A. Knopf, Inc., New York, N.Y.

McCormick, Jack, *The Life of the Forest*, 1966, McGraw-Hill Book Co., Inc., New York, N.Y.

Mitchell, Edwin V. (ed.), *The Art of Walking*, 1934, Loring & Mussey, New York, N.Y.

Muir, John, *A Thousand-mile Walk to the Gulf*, 1916, Houghton Mifflin Co., Boston, Mass.

Myer, William E., *Indian Trails of the Southeast*, 1928, 42nd Annual Report of the Bureau of American Ethnology, Government Printing Office, Washington, D.C.

Niering, William A., *The Life of the Marsh: The North American Wetlands*, 1966, McGraw-Hill Book Co., Inc., New York, N.Y.

O'Kane, Walter Collins, *Trails and Summits of the Green Mountains*, 1926, Houghton Mifflin Co., Boston, Mass.

————, *Trails and Summits of the White Mountains*, 1925, Houghton Mifflin Co., Boston, Mass.

Parris, John, *Roaming the Mountains*, 1955, Citizen-Times Publ. Co., Asheville, N.C.

Peattie, Roderick (ed.), *The Berkshires: The Purple Hills*, 1948, The Vanguard Press, New York, N.Y.

————, *The Great Smokies and the Blue Ridge: the Story of the Southern Appalachians*, 1943, The Vanguard Press, New York, N.Y.

Poole, Ernest, *The Great White Hills of New Hampshire*, 1946, Doubleday & Co., Inc., Garden City, N.Y.

Powell, Levi, *Who Are These Mountain People?* 1966, Exposition Press, Inc., New York, N.Y.

Stupka, Arthur, *Wildflowers in Color*, 1965, Harper & Row, Publishers, New York, N.Y.

Thom, Walter, *Pedestrianism*, 1813, Chalmers & Co., London, England.

Thoreau, Henry, *The Maine Woods*, in *The Writings of Henry David Thoreau, Walden Edition*, 1906, Houghton Mifflin Co., Boston, Mass.

Thornborough, Laura, *The Great Smoky Mountains*, 1937, Thomas Y. Crowell, New York, N.Y.

Tilden, Freeman, *The National Parks, What They Mean to You and Me*, 1951, Alfred A. Knopf, Inc., New York, N.Y.

————, *The State Parks, Their Meaning in American Life*, 1962, Alfred A. Knopf, Inc., New York, N.Y.

Torrey, Raymond H., and others, *New York Walk Book*, latest edition, American Geographical Society, New York, N.Y.

Willey, Benjamin G., *History of the White Mountains*, 1869, Isaac N. Andrews, Boston, Mass.

Index

PHOTOGRAPHIC CREDITS

The American Museum of Natural History: p. 26 (middle). Maurice Broun, Hawk Mountain Sanctuary: p. 92 (middle). William F. Dawson, from the Avery Katahdin Collection, courtesy Appalachian Trail Conference: p. 147. Forest Service, United States Department of Agriculture: title page and pp. 3, 15, 37, 38 (top), 44, 72 (top), 108 (middle), 119, 129, 130 (bottom). Library of Congress: pp. 26 (top), 52 (middle). Massachusetts Department of Commerce: p. 108 (bottom). R. D. Mead: p. 10 (top). National Park Service, United States Department of the Interior: pp. 9, 25, 32, 38 (middle), 51, 52 (bottom), 79 (by E. E. Exline), 91, 92 (top), 139. National Parks Commission of England and Wales: p. 108 (top). North Carolina News Bureau: p. 52 (top). Palisades Interstate Park: p. 92 (bottom). Dick Smith: jacket (front), pp. 10 (middle, bottom), 71, 107, 130 (top, middle), 161. State of New Hampshire, Dick Smith: pp. 59, 72 (bottom), 95. Ann and Myron Sutton: p. 148 (middle, bottom). Michael Sutton: p. 148 (top). Tennessee Conservation Department: p. 38 (bottom). John H. Vondell, courtesy Appalachian Trail Conference: pp. 26 (bottom), 72 (middle).